Understanding and Treating Sex and Pornography Addiction

Understanding and Treating Sex and Pornography Addiction demonstrates why people's lives are being destroyed by compulsive sexual behaviour and what we can do to help them. The book examines the latest research into these conditions and outlines the new integrative C.H.O.I.C.E. Recovery Model, a practical, sex-positive model which incorporates CBT, ACT and psychodynamic theories to help people enjoy lifetime recovery.

This new edition has been updated throughout, with new material covering pornography addiction. ChemSex, internet offending and female sex and love addiction. Written in a clear and informative manner, this book contains support and advice for both the clinician and for those who suffer from sex addiction, and provides tools for securing confident and rewarding recovery.

Understanding and Treating Sex and Pornography Addiction is essential reading for anyone looking to make an enduring recovery from these conditions, as well as for clinicians new to the field and those wanting to update their skills and knowledge.

Paula Hall is a UKCP registered psychotherapist, specialising in sex and porn addiction. She is Clinical Director of the Laurel Centre who provide treatment services around the UK and accredited diploma level training to professionals. She is also founder of the Hall Recovery Course and a founder trustee of ATSAC.

Understanding and Treating Sex and Pornography Addiction

A Comprehensive Guide for People Who Struggle with Sex Addiction and Those Who Want to Help Them

Second edition

Paula Hall

LONDON AND NEW YORK

Second edition published 2019
by Routledge
2 Park Square, Milton Park, Abingdon, Oxon OX14 4RN

and by Routledge
711 Third Avenue, New York, NY 10017

Routledge is an imprint of the Taylor & Francis Group, an informa business

© 2019 Paula Hall

The right of Paula Hall to be identified as author of this work has been asserted by her in accordance with sections 77 and 78 of the Copyright, Designs and Patents Act 1988.

All rights reserved. No part of this book may be reprinted or reproduced or utilised in any form or by any electronic, mechanical, or other means, now known or hereafter invented, including photocopying and recording, or in any information storage or retrieval system, without permission in writing from the publishers.

Trademark notice: Product or corporate names may be trademarks or registered trademarks, and are used only for identification and explanation without intent to infringe.

First edition published by Routledge 2012

British Library Cataloguing in Publication Data
A catalogue record for this book is available from the British Library

Library of Congress Cataloging in Publication Data
Names: Hall, Paula, author.
Title: Understanding and treating sex and pornography addiction : a comprehensive guide for people who struggle with sex addiction and those who want to help them / Paula Hall.
Other titles: Understanding and treating sex addiction
Description: 2nd edition. | Milton Park, Abingdom, Oxon ; New York, NY : Routledge, 2018. | Revision of: Understanding and treating sex addiction / Paul Hall. 2013. | Includes bibliographical references and index.
Identifiers: LCCN 2018012891| ISBN 9780815362265 (hbk) | ISBN 9780815362289 (pbk) | ISBN 9781351112611 (ebk) | ISBN 9781351112604 (mobipocket)
Subjects: LCSH: Sex addiction. | Sex addiction--Treatment.
Classification: LCC RC560.S43 H35 2018 | DDC 616.85/833--dc23
LC record available at https://lccn.loc.gov/2018012891

ISBN: 978-0-8153-6226-5 (hbk)
ISBN: 978-0-8153-6228-9 (pbk)
ISBN: 978-1-351-11263-5 (ebk)

Typeset in Times New Roman
by Taylor & Francis Books

Contents

List of illustrations vii
Acknowledgements ix

Introduction 1

PART I
Understanding sex and porn addiction 3

1 Defining sex and porn addiction 5
2 Assessment 21
3 How addiction starts 33
4 How addiction is maintained and reinforced 49
5 The impact on partners and relationships 61

PART II
Socio cultural differences 71

6 Female sex and love addiction 73
7 Sexual diversities and ChemSex 79
8 Faith communities and spirituality 90
9 Sex offending 96

PART III
The C.H.O.I.C.E. recovery model 105

10 The C.H.O.I.C.E. recovery model: Challenge core beliefs 107
11 The C.H.O.I.C.E. recovery model: Have a vision 118
12 The C.H.O.I.C.E. recovery model: Overcome compulsive behaviours 128
13 The C.H.O.I.C.E. recovery model: Identify positive sexuality 153
14 The C.H.O.I.C.E. recovery model: Connect with others 165
15 The C.H.O.I.C.E. recovery model: Establish confident recovery 176

   Conclusion 190

   Further reading and resources 191

   Index 194

Illustrations

Figures

2.1	The OAT classification model	26
3.1	The BERSC model	35
4.1	Oscillating release/control cycle	50
4.2	The six-phase cycle of addiction	51
4.3	The window of tolerance	56
11.1	The life wheel	125
12.1	The six-phase cycle of addiction	129
12.2	Craig's cycle	131
12.3	Craig's cycle	134
12.4	Craig's cycle	137
12.5	Craig's cycle	138
12.6	Craig's cycle	140
12.7	Craig's cycle	142
13.1	Circle exercise	157
14.1	Concentric circle exercise	170

Tables

1.1	Harmful consequences	16
4.1	Common cognitive distortions	55
12.1	Emotions experienced	139
14.1	SAA 12-Step programme	174

Boxes

10.1	Rock bottoms	109
10.2	Harmful consequences	110
12.1	Identifying triggers	132

12.2	Recognising cognitive distortions	134
12.3	Identifying SUDs	137
12.4	Identifying the positives of acting out	139
12.5	Identifying regrets	140
12.6	Identifying behaviours in the reconstitution phase	141

Acknowledgements

My sincere thanks go to all the people who have helped me to write this revised edition. First, I'd like to thank Dr Meg-John Barker, without whose inspiration this book would never have got started and for her expert guidance on sexual diversity issues. Also David Stuart whose passion and knowledge has inspired us as an organisation to develop our ChemSex services. Many thanks also to Dr Andrew Smith for his help on the sex offending chapter and Gary Wilson for his phenomenal and generously shared research and knowledge on the neuroscience of porn addiction. I'd also like to thank Christine Cartin for her patient and dedicated review of each chapter as well as the whole team at the Laurel Centre for their support in my writing endeavours. Finally I'd like to thank my clients, the many men and women who have put their trust in us to help them build a better life. The 'ordinary guys' and the 'warriors' who have discovered first hand that you can recover from sex and porn addiction, and whose journeys I have had the privilege to be a part of.

Introduction

It's been six years since I wrote the first edition of this book. In some ways much has changed, particularly our understanding of the neuroscience and the growth in concurrent problems such as ChemSex, but in other ways, nothing has changed at all. The terms sex addiction and porn addiction are now widely used, and while professionals continue to debate the name and struggle to find accurate diagnoses, few deny that compulsive sexual behaviours are devastating people's lives.

Human sexuality is a powerful drive, one that we've both celebrated and denigrated throughout history. People who struggle with sex or porn addiction have been taken over by its power, becoming its slave rather than its master. And rather than enjoying a sex life that fits their values and their goals, they're imprisoned by behaviours that damage their self worth and integrity. Sex can build self-esteem and create the closest partner bonds, but it can also break people and relationships in two. Sex can create feelings of both euphoria and shame, pleasure and pain, peace and anguish. Sex is complex and mysterious – surely that's why we love it so much.

How we choose to express our sexuality is a basic human right, but sex and porn addiction robs people of that choice. Like all addictions, what begins as a pursuit of pleasure soon becomes an essential coping mechanism to escape pain and feel normal. Meanwhile relationships are devastated and other meaningful areas of life erode.

This book has been written for people who struggle with sex and porn addiction and for those who care and work with them. Part I covers academic information and provides a guide to understanding the development and function of addiction. Part II is dedicated to specific client communities and offers suggestions on additional considerations when working with these groups. Part III is where you'll find how to recover from sex and porn addiction, including lots of practical and immediately usable self-help information and advice.

The most significant addition to this revised edition is the C.H.O.I.C.E. Recovery Model. The C.H.O.I.C.E. Recovery Model is more than just a structured treatment plan, it's a philosophy; it's not simply a strategy for stopping compulsive behaviours and enduring reluctant sobriety, but a roadmap to establish confident recovery and change your life. The model complements the 12-Steps and provides clinicians with an integrative approach, including strategies from CBT (Cognitive Behavioural Therapy), ACT (Acceptance & Commitment Therapy) and Positive Psychology, as well as psychodynamic, relational and trauma therapy principles. The latest research on neuroscience has been included and there are additional chapters covering female sex and love addiction, ChemSex, sex offending and working with people from sexually diverse communities as well as people of faith.

Sex and porn addiction continues to be a new and emerging field with constantly evolving research and attitudes. Being a pioneer in this field is both hugely exciting and rewarding, and also slightly terrifying. Therefore I encourage all readers to see this book as a foundation for their growth and learning, not a substitute for further training or therapy and support.

It is my sincere hope that this book will give hope to those seeking recovery and help them to see that recovery is a gift; a gift that you can choose, but one that you must choose again, and again and again.

Part I

Understanding sex and porn addiction

Part I has been written primarily for professionals and for those who want an academic overview of what sex and porn addiction is – and what it is not. In Chapter 1 you will find definitions of addiction, including the psychological function addictions play and the latest in neuroscience. Chapter 2 is a practical chapter that explains the different categories of addiction and provides comprehensive assessment tools. In Chapter 3 we look at how addiction gets set up from a biological, emotional, relational, social and cultural perspective. There is also an exploration of common childhood and adolescent themes. We then move on to consider how sex and porn addiction is maintained and reinforced through the six-phase cycle of addiction. We conclude Part I with an overview of the devastation that sex and porn addiction so often has on partners and relationships and the direct impact this can have on addiction recovery.

1 Defining sex and porn addiction

The controversy around sex addiction has not subsided since I wrote the first edition of this book and, like its most recent companion, porn addiction, it continues to be one of the most controversial problems to have entered the public arena in the past 50 years and media interest has not waned. While a growing number of public figures and celebrities battle their condition in the face of public scorn and criticism, others claim it's nothing more than a made-up condition invented to excuse high-flying men who can't control their sex drives. And others sceptically say it's a problem created by sex-hating prudes who moralise sexual diversity and freedom.

Unlike other questionable conditions, the argument over the existence of sex and porn addiction often becomes a moral one, rather than an issue of health. This is undoubtedly because the focus of public and clinical attention is on the word 'sex' or 'porn' rather than on the word 'addiction,' which is the nub of where the problem truly lies. If one considers other addictions that have been thrown into the social ether, such as TV, gambling, shopping, the Internet and even chocolate, they may be vilified but sufferers receive the help they need nonetheless. But when 'sex' is added to the title it becomes a matter of contention, and the first challenge facing many sufferers and the therapists who want to help them is to decide if they really are 'addicted' to sex or porn, or if they simply need to get a grip. Unfortunately, this moral debate over what the condition means and whether it truly exists results in many thousands of sufferers struggling to find help and many clinicians wasting hours of therapeutic time on definition and diagnosis rather than helping the client overcome their problem and move on with their life.

One argument that is proffered against sex and porn addiction's existence is that it seems to have appeared on the social scene so recently, but sex has obviously been available since the dawn of time and erotic images have been found dating from as early as 2000 BC. 'If sex and porn was "addictive" how come it's only happened so recently?' ask some. The answer to this is simple: the Internet, and more recently, the smart phone. The World Wide Web and phone technology have made sexual services, anonymous hook-ups and porn available and accessible to all, and accessible within relative anonymity, hence bypassing the usual social inhibitors.

As millions of sufferers would testify, sex addiction and porn addiction definitely do exist, but like many conditions, they are complex and not easily defined. There are some 'classic' cases that easily fit, yet to be validated, diagnostic criteria but others that do not. Like all addictions, problems may be mild or severe, they may have existed for many years with no apparent cause or they may have been triggered by a particular event and be a relatively recent problem. Or it may be a problem that crops up in someone's life only occasionally. Sex addiction has many guises and encompasses a wide range of sexual behaviours. Most recently, there has been a movement to classify porn addiction separately from sex addiction by both sufferers and the clinical community, but there are many common denominators as we will see in the following chapter. But before we move on, this chapter will explore a variety of definitions and seek to understand why sex and porn addiction causes such emotional, physical and social devastation in people's lives.

What is sex addiction?

The simplest and broadest definition of sex addiction would be that it's a term that describes any pattern of out-of-control sexual behaviour that causes problems in someone's life. Furthermore, it is a pattern of behaviour that cannot be stopped, or does not reliably stay stopped. The type of behaviour does not define addiction, but the dependency on it. Some of the therapeutic community have been critical of writers who list the different sexual practices that may have become compulsive, saying that this pathologises what, for some, are normal and healthy behaviours. This list has often been mistakenly interpreted as a list of signs of addiction, rather than merely a list of behaviours, and has hence been unhelpful. If we were talking about alcohol addiction, we wouldn't list all the beverages that are addictive, it is getting drunk that can be addictive, not gin or whiskey. Similarly, sexual arousal can be addictive, whether that's through watching pornography, having physical sexual encounters, or fantasising about them. It's not the behaviour itself that is the problem *but the relationship to the behaviour*. When we become dependent on something and can't stop doing it, in spite of the problems it's causing in our lives, we generally use the term addiction. Whether that's an accurate label or not will be explored soon.

One of the most common misconceptions about sex and porn addiction is that it's linked to sexual desire. In my clinical experience, backed up by a growing body of research, neither sex nor porn addiction is the same as a high sex drive (Stulholfer et al., 2016). Many of the addicts I've worked with do not get sexual pleasure from what they're doing and it does not satiate their drive. In fact some would go so far as to say they consider themselves to have a very low sex drive or indeed that their addiction has robbed them of their libido.

Whilst their compulsive behaviours are sexual in some respect, the primary motivation is not satiation of sex drive. Sex and porn addiction are not driven by the physical essence of libido but by the psychological need to satisfy a deeper subconscious urge, or to satisfy biological craving in the brain. If you consider a typical porn addict who might spend up to seven or eight hours online at a time, postponing ejaculation for as long as possible, how can we think that their goal is drive satiation? The real motive for such behaviour is escaping from reality and enjoying the aroused brain state, even more than genital stimulation.

In many ways, sex addiction has more in common with eating disorders than it does with other addictions (Goodman, 1993). In one study by Patrick Carnes (1991) 38 percent of his sample had an eating disorder, and in the UK 79 percent of those with another addiction cited eating disorders (Hall, 2013). In the same way that bulimia, anorexia and compulsive over-eating are about an unhealthy relationship with food, sex addiction is an unhealthy relationship with sex. In healthy individuals, both sex and food satisfy a natural, innate and primitive drive, but when the relationship becomes distorted, sex addiction has no more to do with sex drive than eating disorders do with hunger.

However, there are definitely some who suffer with sex or porn addiction who think that they do have a high sex drive and describe their initial motivation for acting out as being a way of meeting their sexual needs. But further investigation and exploration of their feelings often exposes this as mistaken. In the same way as someone with an eating disorder might misinterpret feelings of hunger or fullness, so someone with sex addiction can misinterpret their sexual desire. When sex, porn or food are used compulsively, to the point where it's causing significant problems in someone's life, the function is not to satiate a natural desire but to meet a deeper need. In addiction, the attempt to satiate the deeper need may also be accompanied by cravings and therefore the two can become confused. For example, if someone masturbates every time they feel lonely or bored or angry or sad, after a while they will associate each of those emotions with cravings. Like Pavlov's dogs who salivated every time they heard a bell whether there was food or not, the addict may seek sexual gratification every time they feel a negative emotion whether or not they feel genuine desire.

But is it really an addiction?

Historically the term 'addiction' was only used for chemical addictions – substances such as alcohol, tobacco, heroin and other drugs that cross the blood–brain barrier and alter the brain chemistry.

The notion of an activity being an addiction is a relatively new one but one that is becoming increasingly recognised (Dickson, Derevenksy and Gupta, 2002; Chamberlain et al., 2016, Kraus et al., 2016, Kardefelt-Winther et al., 2017). These are often referred to as 'behavioural' addictions as opposed to 'chemical' addictions. But the term 'addiction' is still an issue for some and consequently you may find people referring instead to video game overuse, pathological gambling, problematic porn use, compulsive debting, problem over-eating and so on. To be honest, the bottom line is that both sufferers and clinicians will use their own favoured term and it doesn't matter what that is as long as help can be offered. But it is precisely the provision of help and its socio-political implications that perpetuate the argument over its name.

How we classify a condition as a society is not just about health, it is also about money and politics. The *Diagnostic and Statistical Manual of the American Psychiatric Association*, or DSM for short, is a widely used and accepted reference tool for recognised mental health conditions. When something is in DSM, it formally exists. And if it formally exists, the public can rightly demand treatment for it. In the world of addictions, there might also be an argument that if a substance or a behaviour has been formally accepted as being 'addictive' then prevention strategies need to be put in place; perhaps there also needs to be controlled access and/or distribution, and compensation may need to be available for innocent sufferers. So if pornography addiction were to officially appear in DSM, just consider how much that could cost the government in treatment provision and policing the industry. Personally, I think as a society we should be taking much more responsibility for the porn industry as we increasingly are with gambling since 'pathological gambling' entered DSM, but the financial ramifications are enormous. Neither sex addiction, nor porn addiction are currently in DSM, though the latest edition, DSM-5 does include substance related and addictive disorders and lists gambling disorder. But another major player in the diagnostics field, used more widely internationally than the DSM, the ICD (International Classification of Diseases), is considering including Compulsive Sexual Behaviour Disorder in its next edition, ICD-11 – scheduled to be published in 2018, (Krueger, 2016).

There are other controversies around DSM and ICD. If a condition is listed then it means it is a problem that needs to be treated or managed, and further researched, rather than a difference to be accepted. And the sufferer may then be saddled with a label that could potentially cause shame and discrimination. It's interesting to note that Asperger's Syndrome was only accepted by DSM in 1994 and homosexuality was not removed until 1973. So up until relatively recently, anyone who was gay was considered to have a mental health problem and there was no support or funding available to help children with Asperger's. Being labelled with a condition or a problem can be both a blessing and a curse. For some it allows them to understand that what they're struggling with is something that's caused problems for many others. The stigma may be removed and energy can be focused on overcoming the problem rather than feeling to blame. But the flipside of this is that for some people, the label becomes a heavy burden under which they feel they have no power or escape. Therefore, the most important thing is to discern what the client wishes to call their problem and what that definition means to them.

Another reason why many health professionals struggle with the label 'addiction' is an assumption that the name implies only one possible treatment approach. Some therapists say they do not subscribe to 'the addiction model' when working with human sexuality, but as we will explore further in this chapter, there are many different 'addiction models,' so it's often difficult to discern what is meant by this. Where alternative treatment approaches are preferred, other names may be suggested, for example hypersexual disorder (Kafka, 2010), Sexual compulsivity (Coleman, 2003), OCSB, (Out of Control Sexual Behaviours), (Braun-Harvey and Vigorito, 2015), or PCSB, (Problem Causing Sexual Behaviour), (Schaefer and Ahlers, 2017). I suspect the terminology list will continue to grow and whilst this may be confusing for some, what is heartening to me, as a therapist, who has been writing about this topic for many years, is that it demonstrates that there is now little doubt that the problem exists.

While the medical and therapeutic communities continue to debate the best name for the problem, the terms 'sex addiction' and 'porn addiction' are becoming increasingly popular on the street and in the media, and many therapists rightly worry that these terms are also being overused, misused and misdiagnosed. According to my survey it seems that the term 'sex addiction' is favoured, with 43 percent of sufferers defining it thus, 22 percent preferring 'love addiction,' 17 percent 'sexual compulsivity' and only 10 percent favouring 'hypersexuality' (Hall, 2013). Whatever the problem is called, what really matters is its definition, not its name.

Variations of sex addiction

Porn addiction

Porn addiction is a subset of sex addiction but sometimes has very different roots to other forms of sex addiction – especially for younger people who have grown up with easy access to internet porn. There is a growing body of research demonstrating the powerful effect of high-speed porn on the brain, which we will explore later in this chapter, but this emerging science has left many people recognising that, unlike traditional sex addiction, porn addiction may be more attributable to brain changes rather than underlying psychological issues. Regrettably many people are not aware they're hooked on porn until it escalates to the point of affecting other areas of life such as relationships, friendships or work. Or until they notice that they can no longer get an erection without using pornography, and sex with a partner no longer holds any appeal. For some the escalation has gone into cybersex, hook ups and visiting sex workers, which may be crossing personal boundaries and breaching fidelity contracts with a partner.

The treatment strategy for porn addiction is fundamentally the same as sex addiction, but with additional emphasis on relapse prevention strategies and building a chosen real-life sexual lifestyle. Greater emphasis also needs to be placed on practical strategies to overcome associated sexual dysfunctions such as PIED (Porn Induced Erectile Dysfunction), which we explore further in Chapter 13.

Love addiction

Love addiction, also known as romance or intimacy addiction, shares many similarities with sex addiction and may or may not include sexual behaviour. The key difference is that it is the process of attraction that creates the buzz rather than any overt sexual behaviour. In reality since many with sex addiction enjoy the chase just as much as the catch, the presentation in therapy may be identical but some clients may prefer the term 'love' addiction to 'sex' addiction as demonstrated by 22 percent of survey respondents (Hall, 2013).

Love addiction is also a term that is often used by women with compulsive sexual behaviours and we explore this much further in Chapter 6. Whatever the behaviour, whether serial affairs, endless flirtations or short-term relationships, the chosen behaviour becomes compulsive and a primary coping mechanism. For people with love addiction, a pattern soon develops that while they appear to be seeking a meaningful relationship where they feel loved, as soon as the relationship matures from the lust and attraction phase into deeper attachment, the love addict moves on. Some people with love addiction find themselves trapped in long-term abusive relationships where they continually seek love. Like someone with sex or porn addiction, in spite of the harmful consequences to their self-esteem and often their safety, they're compulsively driven to seek their partner's affection and positive regard. Research in the field of love addiction is very limited, and hence clinicians should be careful to notice individual treatment requirements (Sussman, 2010).

The function of addiction

To understand any kind of addiction, you need to recognise that it's much, much more than a bad habit that's been developed over a period of time. Addiction has a function, a psychological purpose, (Dodes, 2002). Sex addiction is a coping mechanism, a way of managing life. It is a strategy used to alleviate negative emotions and create positive ones. Some people refer to addiction as an anaesthetising behaviour, a way of numbing out the world. Others refer to addictions as hedonistic behaviour; a way of seeking perpetual pleasure. Often it's both, or at least that's how it starts, but over time the drug of choice, be that sex, cocaine, alcohol or food, creates the very problems you're trying to escape and provides very limited pleasure indeed. What starts as a pursuit of pleasure soon becomes a necessity for feeling normal.

In some respects you could argue that all of human behaviour is based on our desire to increase or elicit a positive feeling state and reduce or eliminate a negative one. We are pre-programmed to seek pleasure and avoid pain as a survival mechanism. Surely that's why there are magazines in doctors' waiting rooms. Rather than focus on our illness, anxiety or boredom, we can distract ourselves with something more interesting. We all have a multitude of techniques and methods for cheering ourselves up and calming ourselves down. Hopefully, most of them are healthy. People with addictions are no different except that their drug of choice has often become their only, and increasingly ineffective, coping mechanism. For someone with sex or porn addiction, rather than finding appropriate and healthy ways of regulating emotion, watching porn, fantasising about sex, having sex has become their primary coping mechanism. It is the only method they have for managing life. Their addiction becomes a buffer between them and the world – a world that is often becoming increasingly unmanageable.

The organisation Sex Addicts Anonymous describe the experience of sexual acting out as 'The Bubble,' (SAA Publications). They say that 'The Bubble,' provides a wall between you and the world and that whilst in it an addict can feel free and liberated, floating above normal life feeling as though nothing can touch them. They can see what's going on in the outside world but it feels detached and unreal; all they can really feel is inside the mystical world of 'The Bubble.' But 'The Bubble' is also a trap and when it bursts and you hit the ground, reality can be overwhelming.

Sex and porn addiction can be viewed as particularly powerful mood-altering drugs because there is such a wide assortment of sexual experiences or porn genres that can elicit a range of emotional responses. In the same way as some drug users will mix and choose between uppers, downers and hallucinogens, the sex or porn user can choose behaviours that will give a range of feeling states. And as science continues to advance, we increasingly understand that those emotions are not purely psychological but are direct products of our brain chemistry. People who are experienced in using sex or porn to modulate emotion can unknowingly, but very effectively, create almost any emotion they wish.

The neurochemistry of addiction

Since the last edition of this book there have been over 50 research papers and professional articles written about the neuroscience underlying sex and porn addiction. What they all have in common is identifying that sex and porn addiction follows a similar neurological pattern to chemical addiction, in terms of the fundamental impact on the brain. Historically much of the doubt around whether or not 'addiction' was an accurate label was based on the lack of evidence that sex and porn could result in the classic hallmarks of addiction, namely tolerance, escalation, increased craving, reduced cognitive control and withdrawal. But that situation is changing.

One common denominator in all addictions is the chemical dopamine, (Robbins and Everitt, 2010). Dopamine is a neurotransmitter that sends messages between the neurons to create neural pathways.

And the more often those pathways are followed, the stronger they become. Dopamine is responsible for motivation and without it the human species would most likely die out. Too little of it can result in depression, whereas too much is linked to addiction. Dopamine makes us 'seek' pleasure and reward and is associated with the experience of craving. Contrary to popular belief, it is not, in itself, responsible for creating the sensation of pleasure, but for driving us to find it. Hence, people with addictions will seek out chemicals and behaviours that often they eventually derive little pleasure from and even less fulfilment. Craving is what defines addiction, and dopamine is responsible for craving. It makes us 'want,' but not necessarily 'enjoy.'

Dopamine is also heightened by novelty and through anticipation and fantasy, which is perhaps why so many of us enjoy cookery programmes as well as porn! What's more, we now know that continual heavy use of addiction-related dopamine pathways reduces their sensitivity, also known as tolerance or desensitisation, and hence greater stimulation is required and the addict seeks greater stimulation to achieve the same effect (Kuhn and Gallinat, 2014, Wery and Billieux, 2016). For a moment, compare sex to food and consider how it would be if the only food available to you was chocolate? Bliss you may think, but imagine eating nothing but your favourite bar week after week after week. It wouldn't take long before you'd become bored and when you did, you'd probably change brand or choose a bar with a higher cocoa count. But as the weeks passed you'd find the pleasure gradually diminishing again. Now imagine that someone offers you an apple and suggests that perhaps you'd enjoy that instead. You take it with keen anticipation, but unbeknown to you, your food pathways have become over-run with the chocolate pathways and the apple tastes completely bland and uninteresting. What would you do?

This is the dilemma of the addicts. Their sexual behaviour or porn use has become the primary way of activating dopamine, and in the meantime their other pleasure pathways have begun to fade away. They may still enjoy listening to music or spending time with friends, but compared to the instant hit they can get from acting out, alternatives are poor substitutes. Each time they activate their reward system through their addiction, the weaker the other pathways become. And the greater the craving becomes for something that can only provide an ever-decreasing measure of pleasure.

Dopamine is also involved in memory processing, and it biases the brain towards events that will provide the reward that it experienced, also known as sensitisation. This also leads to a heightened response to visual cues and what's known as 'attentional bias.' For someone with alcohol addiction that may mean a hyper awareness of bars, but for someone with sex or porn addiction it's a greater reactivity to an attractive person, or porn or something associated with porn use (Voon et al., 2014). For someone with a sex or porn addiction this can make recovery even more challenging and increase feelings of shame as they find themselves unconsciously drawn to anyone fitting their sexual arousal cues.

The neurobiology of addiction encompasses more than the neurochemistry of reward. People with addiction experience difficulties with impulse control, deferring gratification and making judgements about harmful consequences – all processes that involve the frontal cortex of the brain and underlying white matter. These areas of the brain are altered by addiction and since they are still maturing in adolescence, that is why early exposure is believed to be a significant factor in the development of addiction, (Addiction Today, December 2011). Various papers have been written recently about sex and porn addiction that demonstrate reduced cognitive control and decision-making (Love, 2015, Messina et al., 2017), and impaired emotional regulation (Klucken et al., 2016).

There is one area of neuroscience where there is still more research required to validate client experiences and that is what happens when they stop, or try to stop. Withdrawal is a well-known concept within chemical addictions but there has been little investigation of withdrawal symptoms within the field of behavioural addictions, particularly sex and porn. One recent study asked research participants about their experiences of withdrawal from porn and demonstrated that many had experienced negative physical and emotional affect states, (Bothe et al, 2017). However, the reality of withdrawal can be widely seen on the many self-help forums that have sprung up around the Internet and in therapy rooms (Wilson, 2017).

So to conclude, whilst addiction is in part psychological, it is also biological. It is a condition of the brain that disrupts the circuitry and challenges control. Continued chemical misuse or behavioural acting out changes the chemistry of the brain and the brain becomes literally dependent on the chosen drug or activity to feel pleasure and reduce pain. There's more on neurochemistry in later chapters, but for now we'll conclude by looking at the consequences of addiction.

The consequences of sex addiction

Sex or porn addiction can affect every area of a sufferer's life. Initially, the secrecy may seem to provide protection from harmful consequences, and the illusion that 'if no one knows, it won't matter' can perpetuate the behaviour for months or even years. But every choice we make in life comes at a cost and it's only a matter of time before addicts find themselves bankrupt. The sense of loss and destruction that people with sex addiction feel is key to the definition. If there are no negative consequences, then the behaviour may simply be a lifestyle choice. But if life is becoming increasingly unmanageable and unbearable, then the behaviour is more likely to be experienced as a compulsion or an addiction than a choice that comes from free will.

The type of behaviour will dictate the level and extent of damaging consequences. Some may experience significant financial difficulties, others may face legal consequences, and others create workplace difficulties or cause health concerns. A significant proportion have caught sexually-transmitted infections (STIs), suffered from anxiety and depression or had a serious desire to commit suicide as Table 1.1 below indicates. Escalation can result in changes to the arousal threshold (sensitivity to sexual pleasure), often resulting in physical dysfunction such as erectile and ejaculatory problems and also changes in sexual tastes. This is especially true for those with porn addiction and a growing body of research is demonstrating these links. PIED has now been widely written about (Park et al, 2016), as has the way in which compulsive porn can change sexual tastes (Wery and Billieux, 2016).

As well as physical and practical difficulties, all addicts are likely to experience growing problems in their personal relationships and their sense of self. As addiction escalates and an addict increasingly prioritises their acting out behaviour over sexual and intimate relationships with a partner, distance and conflict can grow. These problems are further exacerbated by the secrecy and deceit required to maintain the behaviours and may explode exponentially if the behaviours are discovered or disclosed. Sex addiction is more damaging to relationships than any other addiction because, for many, it breaches a contract of sexual fidelity and trust. As you can see from Table 1.1, 46.5 percent had lost a relationship due to their behaviour. But by far the most damaging consequence of sexual addiction is the impact it has on self-esteem. This is another area where some choose to take sex addiction into the moral realm rather than mental health, assuming the impact on self-esteem is caused by the shame associated with their choice of sexual behaviours. This may indeed be the case for some, but many do not necessarily consider their behaviour to be wrong or shameful. What damages a person's self-esteem is often not the behaviour itself but their lack of control over it. They may not see anything wrong with viewing pornography, but when they're spending eight hours a day or choosing to be online rather than sleep with their

16 *Understanding sex and porn addiction*

Table 1.1 Harmful consequences

Consequence	Actual	Potential
Feelings of shame	70.5%	48.8%
Low self-esteem	65.0%	45.6%
Losing a relationship	46.5%	71.4%
Loss of employment	4.1%	26.3%
Wasted time	62.7%	41.5%
Wasted money	41.9%	35.5%
Debt	14.7%	24.0%
Impaired parenting	14.7%	19.4%
Physical health problems	15.7%	19.8%
Catching an STI	19.4%	47.0%
Mental health problems	49.8%	43.3%
A serious desire to commit suicide	19.4%	–
Sexual dysfunctions	26.7%	22.6%
Legal actions against you	6.0%	17.5%
Press exposure	0.9%	17.5%

Source: (Hall, 2013)

wife or go to their child's school play, then their feelings of self-respect and integrity are damaged. Similarly, someone with sex addiction may not have any issues with the sex trade or prostitution and if, or when, they were single their actions may not have caused them a problem. But once in a committed relationship where they value fidelity and trust, it is the contradiction of their own values that they can't cope with. The dependency on a particular kind of sexual behaviour and the incessant pursuit of it in spite of all the damage it causes, is what damages self-worth. Unfortunately the lower self-worth plummets, the fewer resources someone has to fight addiction. Therefore, as we will see in later chapters, one of the key tasks of the therapist is to help to rebuild self-esteem.

In addition to the 'actual' consequences of sexual addiction, it's also important to remember the 'potential' consequences – in other words, the risks. Whilst some have been luckier than others in what they've had to suffer, living in constant fear and dread that the world could come tumbling down at any second is in itself, a very real negative consequence.

Understanding the impact of sex and porn addiction is key to recognising it as a 'real' problem in people's lives. Whatever you want to call it, however it is defined – it wrecks people's lives and having listened to countless stories of waste and devastation, in my mind there can be no doubt the problems are real. Below is what just a few people said in the survey when asked: 'What has been the worst consequence of your addiction?'

'I lost my wife and my daughter.'

'The ramifications have been far greater than I ever could have imagined. My marriage is still impacted, although I have a loving wife (same one!). I still struggle with shame and depression regarding this as I have still not achieved a healthy sexuality. I still struggle with occasional (fortunately relatively rare) relapses that also have effects on my life and marriage.'

'My addiction has robbed, and continues to rob me of my life. I have become the person I never wanted to be, I have hurt my wife and have a past which would destroy friendships and alienate me even further if it were to come out.'

'Wasted opportunities, a sense of hopelessness and being consumed culminating in near bankruptcy. Not very nice and it still haunts me.'

'Losing the only woman I've ever truly loved.'

'I was caught by my 11 year-old son viewing adult channels on TV which he kept secret for quite a while before being able to confide in his mother.'

'Unwanted pregnancy.'

'Having been in a relationship for 13 years, married for 4, my sexual addiction got too much when I had an affair. My wife found out about it and a lot more stuff came out in the open. I then lost my marriage, causing my 2 children to go through a huge emotional phase in their young lives, which I don't think they will ever get over.'

'Nearly losing my soul mate (and now husband) because I HAD to sleep with some guy whose name I didn't even know.'

'Being arrested.'

'I am a 30 year-old virgin who has never had a girlfriend or dated. Porn has distorted my view of real women and I now think my natural libido is not what it should be. Porn has been a comfort blanket to my anxieties but has at the same time helped to increase them whilst stopping me from facing up to my problems and living my life to the full.'

'Clinical depression. My ex-husband finding out after 5 years, that I was having an affair. Frequent tearful visits to GUM [genitourinary medicine] clinics. I contracted an STI after being raped in my teens and I still put myself at risk sometimes.'

'Wanting to commit suicide.'

'Losing child.'

'Depression, isolation.'

'Police warning, self-loathing, terror of catching an STI if something has gone wrong and the absolute fear of losing those I love.'

'Shame … risk of infections, inability to have a relationship.'

'Failure of two marriages, daughter in drug rehab, son who does not talk to me.'

References

Addiction Today, December (2011) The Latest Definition of Addiction from ASAM (American Association of Addiction Medicine).

Bothe, B., Toth-Kiraly, I., Zsila, A., Griffiths, M.D., Demetrovics, Z., & Orosz, G. (2017) The development of the problematic pornography consumption scale (PPCS). *The Journal of Sex Research*, 1–12, Published online 6 March 2017.

Braun-Harvey, D. & Vigorito, M.A. (2015) *Treating Out of Control Sexual Behaviour: Rethinking Sex Addiction*, New York: Springer Publishing Company.

Carnes, P. (1991) *Don't call it love: Recovery from sexual addiction*, New York: Bantam.

Chamberlain, S.R., LochnerC., Stein, D.J., Goudriaan, A., Jankevan Holste, R., Zoharf, J., & Grant, J.E. (2016) Behavioural addiction – A rising tide? *European Neuropsychopharmacology*, 26(5): 841–855.

Coleman, E. (2003) Compulsive sexual behaviour: what to call it, how to treat it, *SIECUS report*, 31(5): 12–16.

Dickson, L., Derevensky, J., & Gupta, R. (2002) The prevention of gambling problems in youth: A conceptual framework. *Journal of Gambling Studies*, 18: 97–159.

Dodes, I. (2002) *The Heart of Addiction: A New Approach to Understanding and Managing Alcoholism and Other Addictive Behaviours*, William Morrow.

Goodman, A. (1993) Diagnosis and treatment of sexual addiction. *Journal of Sex & Marital Therapy*, 19: 225–251.
Hall, P. (2013) *Understanding & Treating Sex Addiction*, Routledge, London.
Kafka, M.P. (2010) Hypersexual disorder: a proposed diagnosis for DSM-V, *Archives of Sexual Behaviour*, 39: 377–400.
Kardefelt-Winther, D., Heeren, A., Schimmenti, A., van Rooij, A., Maurage, P., Carras, M., Edman, J., Blaszczynski, A., Khazaal, Y., & Billieux, J. (2017) How can we conceptualize behavioural addiction without pathologizing common behaviours? *Addiction*, 112: 1709–1715.
Klucken, T., Wehrum-Osinsky, S., Schweckendiek, J., Kruse, O., & Stark, R. (2016) Altered Appetitive Conditioning and Neural Connectivity in Subjects With Compulsive Sexual Behavior, *The Journal of Sexual Medicine*, 13(4): 627–636.
Kraus, S.W., Voon, V., Kor, A., & Potenza, M.N. (2016) Searching for clarity in muddy water: Future considerations for classifying compulsive sexual behavior as an addiction, *Addiction*, 2113–2114.
Krueger, R.B. (2016) Diagnosis of hypersexual or compulsive sexual behavior can be made using ICD-10 and DSM-5 despite rejection of this diagnosis, American Psychiatric Association, *Addiction*, 111: 2110–2111. doi: 10.1111/add.13366.
Kuhn, S., & Gallinat, J. (2014) Brain structure and functional connectivity associated with pornography consumption: The brain on porn, *Journal of the American Medication Association Psychiatry*, 71(7): 827–834.
Love, T., Laier, C., Brand, M., Hatch, L., & Hajela, R. (2014) Neuroscience of Internet Pornography Addiction: A Review and Update, *Behavioural Sciences*, 5(3): 388–433.
Messina, B., Fuentes, D., Tavares, H., Abdo, H.N., & Scanavino., M. (2017) Executive functioning of sexually compulsive and non-sexually compulsive men before and after watching an erotic video. *The Journal of Sexual Medicine*, 14(3): 347–354.
Park, B.Y., Wilson, G., Berger, J., Christman, M., Reina, B., Bishop, F., Klam, W.P., & Doan, A.P. (2016) Is Internet Pornography Causing Sexual Dysfunctions? A Review with Clinical Reports, *Behavioural Sciences*, 6(3): 17.
Robbins, T., & Everitt, B. (eds) (2010) *The Neurobiology of Addiction*, Oxford University Press, Oxford.
Schaefer, G.A., & Ahlers, C.J. (2017) Sexual Addiction, Terminology, Definitions and Conceptualisations, in Birchard, T. & Benfield, J. (eds) *The Routledge International Handbook of Sexual Addiction*, Routledge, London: pages 21–26.
Sex Addicts Anonymous, *The Bubble: An Analogy about Sex Addiction*, SAA Publications, London.
Stulhofer, A., Jurin, T., & Briken, P. (2016) Is high sexual desire a facet of male hypersexuality? Results from an online study, *Journal of Sexual and Marital Therapy*, 42(8): 665–680.
Sussman, S. (2010) Love Addiction: Definition, Etiology, Treatment, *Sexual Addiction & Compulsivity*, 17: 1.

Voon, V., Mole, T.B., Banca, P., Porter, L., Morris, L., & Mitchell, S. *et al.* (2014) Neural correlates of sexual cue reactivity in individuals with and without compulsive sexual behaviours, *PloS ONE*, 9*(*7*)*. *Online.* Available at http://journals.plos.org/plosone/article/asset?id=10.1371%2Fournal.pone.0102419.PDF (Accessed November 2017).

Wéry, A., & Billieux, J. (2016) Online sexual activities: An exploratory study of problematic and non-problematic usage patterns in a sample of men, *Computers in Human Behaviour*, 56: 257–266.

Wilson, G. (2017) *Your Brain on Porn, Internet pornography and the emerging science of addiction*, Commonwealth Publishing, UK.

2 Assessment

You cannot treat a problem until you know what it is. In every area of psychology and medicine, accurate assessment is essential and never more so than in sex and porn addiction where confusion abounds. Misdiagnosis is common among people with sex and porn addiction and the focus of the work often becomes the cause or the consequence, rather than the addiction itself. But this isn't necessarily the fault of the clinician.

Many people with sex or porn addiction come for counselling or sexual health support because of the anxiety or depression that the problem is causing. Or because of the impact it is having on their relationship or on their sex life or, with younger porn addicts, on their studies and social life. Although the situation is beginning to change as sex and porn addiction become more widely recognised, there are still many who will initially seek help for a secondary issue. For many people it's too painful or risky to talk about their sexual acting out or their porn use so instead they will seek help for the consequences without openly acknowledging the cause, if indeed they're aware of it. Others may be aware that their compulsive behaviour has originated from a childhood wound and they come for help with this and only hint at the extent of their current addiction. While the cause and the consequence both need to be worked on, unfortunately the addiction is too often left to continue to thrive. As we will see in Part III of this book, it's essential that treatment is seen within the context of working with the whole person, and therefore the cause, effect and addiction need to be considered.

Assessment is also essential for breaking through denial. Accepting that you've got a problem with sex and/or porn is not easy for most and while some people may come for counselling with an inkling that they may have a problem, many will struggle to accept the severity. A formal assessment process can help clients to explore their situation in an objective way and come to a conclusion for themselves. It's essential that therapists do not try to force a diagnosis of sex or porn addiction, as this can prevent someone seeking the help they need at a later date.

But having said all that, not everyone wants a 'label' for their problems. Clinicians need to be sensitive to what impact a formal assessment might have on a client. It's important to ask clients how finding out you have sex or porn addiction will help them. Will a name help to reduce the shame they feel about their behaviour or make it worse? Will it be a comfort, or a hindrance? Will it increase or decrease their motivation to overcome the problems they're facing? Whether a client chooses a formal assessment process and the consequence of a label or not, assessing their motivation to change is essential to establish the focus for work.

The assessment process

Assuming a client is happy to engage in a formal assessment process, the following three assessment tools can be offered. The first will establish if the behaviour might be considered compulsive; the second how severe the addiction is; and the third what category the addiction may fall into and what core issues need to be addressed to secure full recovery. We will look at each in order now.

Questionnaire 1: Do I have a sex or porn addiction?

1 Does your sexual behaviour or porn use have a 'significant' negative impact on other areas of your life such as maintaining or forming relationships, spending time with family and friends, concentrating on work or studies, getting into debt, risking your mental or physical health, maintaining personal and legal boundaries?
2 Do you find yourself struggling to concentrate on other areas of your life because you are preoccupied with thoughts and feelings about your porn use or sexual behaviour?
3 Have you noticed that you need more and more stimuli or risk, or that you are watching what you would describe as more extreme porn, in order to achieve the same level of arousal and excitement?
4 Have you tried to limit your porn use or sexual behaviours, or stop all together, but repeatedly failed?

If the answer is 'Yes' to all of these questions, then someone is likely to be struggling with sex or porn addiction and the following questionnaire will help to identify how severe the problem is. If there are strong feelings of ambivalence this may be because someone is still in denial of their problem or it may be that their difficulty is mild. Again, the severity questionnaire will help to clarify.

Questionnaire 2: Measuring severity

The following questions have been taken from the SASAT, (Sex Addiction Severity Assessment Tool), which is now widely used in many organisations around the UK. Some prefer to give the questionnaire to clients to complete alone and then talk through their answers; others prefer to use it during a session. The SASAT can help to elicit further information about the kinds of sexual behaviours engaged in and the frequency – for many clients, asking these questions as part of formal assessment can help to reduce shame as it demonstrates that these behaviours are commonplace. There are also questions that help to establish if addictive or compulsive behaviours are long-standing or may have roots in the family of origin as well as providing more details on the impact of the behaviour. The SASAT is used with a numerical rating scale in some organisations to enable clinicians to establish severity and signpost to relevantly trained treatment services, but please note that this tool has not yet been validated − if there's an eager researcher out there reading this, please do get in touch!

1. How long have you been struggling with the behaviours that have brought you here today?
2. Have you had similar difficulties in the past with other types of sexual behaviours?
3. Do you currently, or have you in the past, struggled with any other addictions, compulsive behaviours or eating disorders? Such as drug or alcohol addiction, compulsive gambling, gaming, work or exercise?
4. Has anyone in your family currently, or in the past, struggled with any addictions, compulsive behaviours or eating disorders such as those listed above?
5. Over an average 6 months of active addiction, how often have you engaged in the behaviours shown in the following table:

	Never	Only occasionally	Some-times	Often	Most or all the time
Using pornography *(including internet, smart phone, TV, DVDs, magazines)*	☐	☐	☐	☐	☐
Visiting sex workers *(including prostitutes, masseurs, strip clubs)*	☐	☐	☐	☐	☐
Cyber sex *(including chat sites, dating sites, adult apps, hook up sites, web cams)*	☐	☐	☐	☐	☐
Telephone sex or live TV adult channels	☐	☐	☐	☐	☐
Sex with strangers/one night stands/cruising/sex parties	☐	☐	☐	☐	☐
Multiple affairs/casual sex/swinging	☐	☐	☐	☐	☐
Do you find yourself pre-occupied with either planning for, fantasising about or recovering from your sexual behaviours?	☐	☐	☐	☐	☐
Do your behaviours have a negative impact on your relationship? Or your ability to start a relationship?	☐	☐	☐	☐	☐
Do your behaviours have a negative impact on your family, friends, work, relaxation time or finances?	☐	☐	☐	☐	☐
Do your sexual behaviours leave you feeling isolated from friends and family?	☐	☐	☐	☐	☐
Do you engage in sexual behaviours in spite of potential risk of physical or emotional harm to yourself or others?	☐	☐	☐	☐	☐
How often have you engaged in your behaviours to relieve depressed feelings/low mood or boredom?	☐	☐	☐	☐	☐
How often have you engaged in your behaviours to alleviate stress and stressful feelings?	☐	☐	☐	☐	☐
How often have you tried to stop your behaviours?	☐	☐	☐	☐	☐
Have you ever felt suicidal as a result of your sexual behaviours?	☐	☐	☐	☐	☐

The final question is of course critical. Whether the behaviour is an addiction or not, and whether the client agrees or not, this is a severe problem if a client finds themselves often considering suicide.

Classifications of sex addiction

Before we move on to the final assessment tool, let me provide a brief explanation. In the same way as there are currently no formal definition and diagnosis criteria for sex addiction, there is also no clearly defined classification system. The profile of the 'typical' sex addict is changing. Fifty years ago it would only have been those with significantly dysfunctional backgrounds who would have been driven enough to pursue their sexual anaesthetic. But now there's an increasing number of clients with only minor historic difficulties who stumble upon the joys of sex and pornography and become hooked. In the survey (Hall, 2013), 44 percent of respondents said they had no experience of childhood abuse or trauma and 26.5 percent of respondents had never experienced any of the well-recognised attachment related issues. As clinicians it's important that we recognise this distinct client group and ensure we don't attempt to pathologise their past by trying to find trauma and attachment issues that either do not exist or are not relevant. There are few of us in life who have completely escaped trauma or a bit of negative parenting. And there are few of us who won't have used sex and relationships as an anaesthetic when life is hard. But someone with an addiction stays stuck in this pattern of behaviour and the reasons for this are often complex and ultimately the client must decide on whether or not their behaviour is out of control.

The OAT Model, (Hall, 2013) is now widely used to help identify the range of ways that someone might fall into addiction. Broadly speaking, addiction is Opportunity-induced, Attachment-induced or Trauma-induced and often a combination of two or all three.

As you can see in Figure 2.1, opportunity is present in each of the three classifications of addiction. In addition, a sufferer may have problems with attachment, trauma or attachment and trauma.

Opportunity-induced addiction

Whatever a client's history and individual circumstances, if there was no opportunity for viewing porn or sexual acting out, it would not happen. The reality of the Western world today is that 'opportunity' is everywhere and people, with or without a background of trauma and/or attachment difficulties, can now indulge their sexual desires and run the risk of becoming addicted.

Figure 2.1 The OAT classification model

The Internet has turned pornography and cyber sex into what's known as Supernormal Stimuli. This term was first coined in the 1930s to describe the many different substances and situations that trigger our instinctive impulses beyond their original evolutionary purpose. One common example of this is sugar. Humans have a natural craving for sweet foods, which, in hunter/gatherer days, would have given us much-needed bursts of energy. But in our modern world, filled with an endless variety of sugary substances, that natural desire for sugar has resulted in a global obesity epidemic. Similarly, Mother Nature gave us a primal drive to seek out sexual partners and be aroused by visual cues – a drive required to survive. But the Internet now feeds our senses with visual stimuli and sexual opportunities, and hence pornography and cybersex, like sugar, have become Supernormal Stimuli and our brains must work harder to control and manage our primal appetite.

There appear to be common characteristics that predispose some people to be more easily influenced by the proliferation of sexual experience, mostly linked to healthy emotional regulation and adolescent sexual development, but it may be more a case of bad luck than bad judgement that leads so many down the road to addiction.

Attachment-induced addiction

'Addiction is an attachment disorder' is a common refrain among addiction specialists and this is undoubtedly true in a significant number of cases (Flores, 2004). But to assume that childhood attachment issues are always at the root of the problem is overly simplistic. We know that when a child forms a secure attachment with their primary care giver they are more likely to grow into an adult with positive self-esteem who is able to tolerate and manage strong emotions and mild trauma (Potter-Efron, 2006). But if positive parenting has been unreliable or absent a child is more likely to fear negative feelings and turn to an addiction for comfort during times of trouble rather than to a person.

Someone with an attachment-induced addiction will be unconsciously using their behaviour as a way of soothing relational pain such as fears of rejection or suffocation, loneliness or low self-esteem. The behaviour may be a way of getting close to people in a controlled manner or alternatively a way of creating or maintaining distance from an otherwise committed relationship. For example, a happily married man with a history of attachment problems may use pornography or sex workers as a way of avoiding full commitment and intimacy with his wife. Or someone who has never been in a committed relationship may use their addiction as a way of experiencing physical intimacy.

Trauma-induced addiction

The link between trauma and addiction is well documented (Carruth, 2011). Addiction may on some occasions be directly triggered by a traumatic event, for example, bereavement, physical assault or sudden illness might instigate a habit of using masturbation for comfort that then leads to an addiction. Or sometimes a traumatic event, or events, occur in childhood, and sex becomes a way of coping with the subsequent emotional and physical fallout. Significant trauma can also have a direct impact on the structure of the brain and the repetitive nature of the compulsive behaviour can become a way of soothing a hyperactive amygdala and limbic system and reduce symptoms of hyper arousal and hypo arousal (Fowler, 2006; Fisher, 2007).

Someone with a trauma-induced addiction is most likely to use the behaviour to self soothe difficult emotions and the chosen behaviour may in some way replicate the initial trauma. For example, someone who's experienced significant physical abuse may become addicted to BDSM practices (Birchard, 2011). On the outside a trauma-induced addict may appear self controlled, calm and high functioning but inside there may be resonance of anxiety and stress. Someone with a trauma-induced addiction is also more likely than any other to experience powerful feelings of anxiety about giving up the behaviour.

It's possible that some people with a trauma-induced addiction may have never considered that their trauma may be linked to their addiction and may not mention anything about it in therapy. Assuming the trauma didn't happen within the family of origin, childhood may be otherwise happy, and adult relationships may be reasonably well balanced and functional. However, trauma that was experienced very early in life or was suffered at the hands of a primary care giver may present with attachment issues too. Indeed, early traumatisation may make it almost impossible for children to form healthy attachment bonds (Potter-Efron, 2006).

Defining the type of sex addiction

The questions in this section can help you to begin to determine if an addiction is attachment, trauma or opportunity-induced. The questions are primarily about childhood and adolescence, a time when addiction is often set up. There is more about this in the next chapter.

Opportunity-induced addiction

1 Did you have access to pornography from what you would describe as an 'early age?'
2 Did you experience encouragement or influence to be sexually active, either with others or through masturbation, from parents or mentors?
3 Before the age of 16, were you able to access Internet pornography, in private, almost any time you desired?
4 Has Internet access and broadband significantly increased your unwanted sexual behaviours?
5 Did you use pornography more than 80 per cent of the time when you masturbated during adolescence?
6 Have you had easy and regular access to sexual partners, sex workers or other sexual activities, for example, because of where you lived or worked, through travel or through a particular work or social culture?
7 Have you had the financial resources to pay for your sexual behaviours?
8 Has it been easy for you to keep your sexual behaviours hidden from others?

Attachment-induced addiction

1 Were you separated from your parents or any other key people in your life when you were growing up, for example through adoption, fostering, bereavement or divorce/separation?
2 Did you experience any significant periods of separation from your family, for example, through hospitalisation, a parent working away or attending boarding school?
3 Did you experience regular threats of separation, abandonment or rejection as a child?

4   Did you experience impaired parenting, for example, as a result of family illness, disability, alcoholism, imprisonment, domestic abuse or extreme poverty?
5   Did you experience neglectful parenting, for example, receiving little or no attention, affection or affirmation?
6   Did you feel isolated from your family and not accepted, perhaps due to your gender or sexual orientation, or because your birth was not planned?
7   Did you and your family move home more often than you would perceive as 'average'?

Trauma-induced addiction

1   Did you experience any form of physical abuse in childhood, for example excessive physical punishment from your parents, carers, teachers, siblings or peers?
2   Did you experience any on-going emotional abuse in childhood, for example aggression, threats, name calling or bullying?
3   Did you experience any sexual abuse in childhood, for example being touched inappropriately or being made to touch someone else inappropriately, or being made to touch yourself sexually and being watched or being forced to watch someone else being sexual or forced to watch sexually explicit material?
4   Were you ever sexually assaulted?
5   Were you ever physically assaulted?
6   Were there ever any incidents of domestic violence in your home?
7   Did you experience any traumatic losses in your childhood or adolescence, for example bereavement, sudden disability or illness of someone close to you?
8   Have you at any stage in your life witnessed disturbing scenes of violence, brutality, loss or suffering, or feared for your life or safety?

Understanding which category an addiction falls under is not simply a case of counting up the 'Yes's' because each statement does not necessarily carry the same weight. Someone may tick a lot of boxes in the 'attachment' category but self-awareness and subsequent healthy relationships may have dealt with many of those wounds. Therefore, childhood attachment difficulties may contribute to the addiction but the main activator may be a particularly traumatic event that happened in teens. Whenever questionnaires are used in assessment, it's essential to explore not just the facts revealed but also what they mean to the individual. The information elicited by assessment can then be used as a guide rather than a template.

Additional considerations in assessment

Assessing adolescents

Identifying sex or porn addiction in adolescence poses a number of difficulties since many of the identifying factors might be described as 'normal' adolescent behaviours. Adolescence is a time of change and experimentation and hence many young people engage in sexual acts that are risky or which they later regret. And while hormones are raging and sex is a novelty, it's common for thoughts of sex and the pursuit of sex to feel all encompassing. Clinicians and concerned adults should also be aware of changing cultural norms and not jump to conclusions about behaviours that they find challenging. It's been suggested that diagnosing adolescent sex addiction requires a more detailed assessment, in particular about the role of masturbation and fantasies and adults should suspend assumptions that young people cannot become addicted because the behaviour can't have existed for long enough (Griffin-Shelley, 2002).

Many clinicians confirm that sex addiction in adolescence is a problem, although it's often not recognised by their clients until later in life (Sussman, 2007). Within my 2012 survey 29 percent reported that the problem began between the ages of 17 and 25, 31 percent between 11 and 16, and 8.8 percent under the age of 10 (Hall, 2013). And according to the ongoing survey conducted by www.sexaddictionhelp.co.uk, over 40 percent of the 20,000 respondents said the problem started under the age of 16. With the increasing access to the Internet, more young people are able to intentionally seek pornography, although this does not necessarily mean they will develop a problem (Ybarra and Mitchell, 2005); however, it's clear that some are. A survey conducted by BBC Newsbeat in 2011 reported that 25 percent of respondents said they were worried about their porn use and a report conducted by NSPCC Childline in 2015, stated that up to a tenth of 12–13 year olds feared they were addicted to porn (Howse, 2015). This is an area that needs considerably more research, both from the perspective of offering support and treatment for young people with sex and porn addiction, but also to provide education and preventative work.

Assessment with gender, sexual and relationship diverse clients

This is explored in length in Chapter 7, but is worthy of mention here also. It's essential in assessment that therapists are aware of any heteronormative bias that they may have. As explored in Chapter 1, sex and porn addiction is not defined by the behaviour, but by the dependency and inability to stop in spite of harmful consequences. Misdiagnosis amongst diverse communities risks pathologising healthy sexual expression and hence therapists must remain mindful of other explanations for presentation for therapy from these client groups. Even if a behaviour is experienced as unwanted, addiction may not be the cause and alternative therapy approaches should be thoroughly explored.

Assessment and other addictions

Numerous studies highlight the prevalence of cross-addiction and co-occurring addictions (Carnes et al., 2005) and, in the UK, 58 percent of sex addicts had experienced other addictions or compulsive behaviours (Hall, 2013). This is particularly prevalent in the ChemSex community that we explore in Chapter 7.

If a client presents with other addictions, such as to alcohol or drugs, especially if these are concurrent, then therapists need to ensure they are suitably trained to work with the chemical dependency as well as sexual compulsivity. A suitable risk assessment needs to be undertaken, with referral to other agencies for detox if appropriate.

Assessment and mental health disorders

It is common for clients to present with other mental health disorders, such as anxiety, depression, OCD (obsessive compulsive disorder), bipolar or personality disorders. Where these are present, assessment needs to take into consideration the current treatment regimes for these other issues and whether co-working with a mental health professional or referral would be a better option. This is another area where recognising what may be cause or consequence is essential and the untrained therapist who works solely on the addiction, or on the mental health problem, may inadvertently exacerbate the other.

References

Birchard, T. (2011) Sexual Addiction and the Paraphilias, *Sexual Addiction & Compulsivity*, 18: 3.

Carnes, P., Murray, R., & Charpentier, L. (2005) Bargains with chaos: Sex addicts and addiction interaction disorder, *Sexual Addiction & Compulsivity*, 12: 79–120.

Carruth, B. (2011) *Psychological Trauma and Addiction Treatment*, Routledge, London.

Fisher, J. (2007) *Addictions and Trauma Recovery*, Basic Books, New York.
Flores, P.J. (2004) *Addiction as an Attachment Disorder*, Aronson, Maryland.
Fowler, J. (2006) Psychoneurobiology of co-occurring Trauma and Addictions, *Journal of Chemical Dependency Treatment*, 8(2).
Griffin-Shelley, E. (2002) *Adolescent Sex and Love Addicts: Clinical Management of Sex Addiction*, Routledge, London.
Hall, P. (2013) *Understanding and Treating Sex Addiction*, Routledge, London.
Howse, P. (2015) Pornography addiction worry for tenth of 12 to 13 year olds Education and Family, *BBC News*. Online. Available at www.bbc.com/news/education-32115162 (Accessed November 2017).
Potter-Efron, R. (2006) Attachment, Trauma and Addiction, in Carruth, B. (ed) *Psychological Trauma and Addiction Treatment*, Routledge, London, pages 71–87.
Sussman, S. (2007) Sex Addiction among Teens: A Review, *Sexual Addiction & Compulsivity*, 14: 4.
Ybarra, M.L., & Mitchell, K.J. (2005) Exposure to Internet Pornography among Children and Adolescents: A National Survey, *Cyber Psychology & Behaviour*, 8: 5.

3 How addiction starts

'Why have I become addicted?' is perhaps one of the most common questions I'm asked when someone has recognised and acknowledged that they have a problem. The question is often asked in a state of confusion and with urgency as someone attempts to make sense of what can initially feel like an overwhelming and daunting diagnosis. 'Am I mentally ill?' 'Is it because of something I've done?' 'Is this because I was abused?' – the questions often come thick and fast and beneath the desperate desire to seek understanding is a simpler question – 'Can I change?' Before beginning to explore how sex addiction starts, it's important to offer reassurance that whatever the cause, the problem can be overcome. This is especially important when someone has suffered childhood abuse and has already made a link between that and their current behaviour. For someone with a trauma-induced addiction, it's easy to assume that the damage is already done. But whatever the category of addiction, developing a greater understanding of the underlying causes is essential as it allows any negative messages or behavioural patterns that may have been established to be challenged and healthier coping strategies can then be developed.

There is of course no single or simple answer to why someone develops an addiction, whether it's attachment-induced, trauma-induced or purely opportunity-induced as outlined in the previous chapter. Understanding how something came to be is almost always a complex interweaving of many different factors, whether that's understanding how you got into the job you do or why a car crash happened. There are always multiple factors to be taken into consideration, many of which are dependent on another.

For example, if you're an acclaimed violinist, chances are that your love of music started in early childhood, and from an early age you learned that you had an innate musical talent. Perhaps your parents encouraged you to listen to and play music, and your passion was nurtured and your efforts and accomplishments praised. Negative events may have played a role too. Perhaps your first violin was inherited from your late grandfather who you miss very much, but who inspired you to commit to the instrument. If you also had the financial resources to pay for lessons and perhaps go and see live concerts to feed your ambition, and your local secondary school happened to be known for its excellent music teaching, then your journey to success had an excellent start. However, changing just a few key factors or introducing a discriminating wild card such as illness or parental separation might have changed your direction and set you on a very different path. Understanding the fragility of a life path is important because it can help us to understand why people with almost identical histories might develop very differently. It can also help us not to place undue blame or regret on one single incident or circumstance, something that is especially important in sex and porn addiction where shame can play such a crucial role.

When looking at the causes of sex and porn addiction, it's important to ask two questions. The first is, 'why does someone become an addict?' and the second, 'why did they become addicted to that particular sexual behaviour or porn type?' The answers to the first question generally reside in childhood, whereas the answer to the second usually lies around the time of puberty and adolescence. There are a number of common patterns in the histories of people with addictions, whether that's to a chemical or a behaviour, but the causes of choosing online or offline sex, rather than alcohol, drugs or gambling, are tied up with sexual development and also availability and accessibility.

Each of these causes is best explored through an integrative model that takes into account every area of a person's life. The BERSC model (Hall, 2017) (see Figure 3.1) is an expansion on the biopsychosocial model first theorised by psychiatrist George Engel in 1977. This model allows a framework through which to consider someone's unique biological make-up, their emotional predispositions and scripts, relational experiences from childhood through to adult couple relationships, the societal factors that influence our lives and also any relevant cultural factors such as religion, ethnicity, sexual identity and orientation, peer groups and work environments. This holistic framework is important for minimising shame and developing an accurate understanding of the factors that uniquely contribute to each person's addiction. The BERSC model also encourages a comprehensive treatment approach that focuses on the client's individual circumstances and needs rather than favouring any singular therapeutic approach.

The following pages in this chapter will explore the most common causes of sex addiction within the categories of attachment-, trauma- and

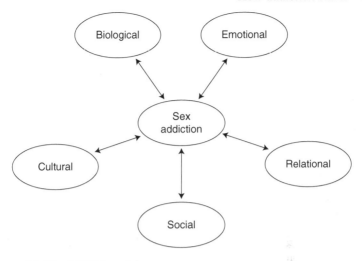

Figure 3.1 The BERSC model

opportunity-induced and will cover each element of the BERSC model. We will start with opportunity since, without this, sex and porn addiction would not exist – in the same way as if our acclaimed violinist had never heard or owned a violin, he would never have got where he is today. Almost everyone will be familiar with the causes under the 'opportunity-induced' heading, while others will additionally identify with the causes under the headings of trauma and attachment.

Opportunity-induced addiction

Pornography and potential sexual partners are available anywhere and everywhere. On the streets, in bars and clubs and in the privacy of your own home. The Internet has allowed unlimited and anonymous access to either viewing or engaging in any and every kind of sexual activity that our hearts and loins might desire. There are ample free online sexual activities to explore and there are no public health warnings or obvious negative consequences – until of course, you're hooked. Imagine how our world might be if heroin was available like this? How many more of us might follow our curiosity and sample the wares? If you had no idea that it could damage you or other areas of your life, what would stop occasional recreational use escalating into an addiction? In the survey, one in five people said not knowing sex could be addictive was the most influential factor in becoming addicted and one in three cited easy access to sexual opportunities, (Hall, 2013). In an on-going online survey at www.sexaddictionhelp.co.uk, 38 percent of the 619 respondents who had completed the OAT questionnaire, described their addiction as opportunity-induced.

No addiction can exist without opportunity, and in the absence of adequate education and advice, people will experiment, explore and take risks that they didn't know were there. It is the nature of humanity that we like new and pleasurable experiences and which ones we choose to follow and for how long is dependent on our temperament and our life experience. We will go on to explore these in a moment, but it's important to highlight that society is responsible for some of the causes of sex and porn addiction. I am not trying to suggest that we should enforce some kind of sexual prohibition or censor all pornographic material, but in the same way as we teach and encourage healthy eating and responsible drinking, so we should establish appropriate public information for safe sexuality – especially for our young people – information that allows people to make informed choices rather than blindly stumbling into addiction as so many find they do. Sexual experimentation is natural, healthy and commonplace, and it's my personal belief that all of us have a predisposition towards addiction, so with all these sexual opportunities available to us all, why is it that only some get trapped? I hope the following will help to answer the question.

Developing self-control

When we talk about self-control and its role in addiction, it's important not to reduce this simply to impulse control. It's true that many addicts struggle with impulse control, especially in the early days of their acting out behaviour, but maintaining a porn habit or sex addiction usually takes meticulous planning and organisation. Furthermore, when working with porn addiction, it may be poor impulsive control that gets you online, but to still be there 4 hours later is something else. In the context of addiction, developing self-control means being able to make decisions and control one's behaviour based on sound judgement of your individual needs and any resulting consequences.

We begin to learn self-control in childhood and there are two ways in which parents can fail to teach this essential skill. The first, which is most common in addiction, is to have a strict and rigid home environment where a child is never allowed to make decisions for themselves (Carnes, 1991). In the survey 60 percent of respondents described their family background as strict and controlling (Hall, 2013). There is either a spoken or unspoken dictate that the parents know what's best for the child.

Consequently it is the parents' will that is imposed, leaving no space for a child's will and willpower to develop. The consequence of over strict parenting is often an adolescent or adult who refuses to be controlled by anybody or anything other than the self, regardless of the consequences. This rebellious attitude might be overtly demonstrated in someone who breaks all the rules their parents held or it might be a quieter rebellion where the behaviour is acted out in secret.

The second way that parents may fail to teach control is by having a home with few or no boundaries (26 percent in the survey, Hall, 2013). A child who grows up with a sense that their parents never knew where they were or what they were up to, or that there were no rules to break, often grows up without ever knowing the benefits of moderating their behaviour.

Managing difficult feelings

Another essential lesson that parents need to teach is how to manage difficult emotions. None of us get through life without experiencing pain and hardship and therefore we all need to develop healthy coping mechanisms that will enable us to soothe the pain without creating further problems.

Many people with addiction describe a family of origin where there was either no expression of emotion or emotions were expressed with such intensity that they were frightening or even dangerous. Seventy-seven percent in the survey said they didn't learn how to manage their emotions and problems healthily (Hall, 2013). Either of these extremes can result in someone who has no model of how to healthily experience anger, sadness, frustration, loneliness, loss and so on and so on. Instead these emotions become buried and soothed with sex. And please note, porn in particular can be a highly effective way of managing painful emotions, and consequently someone with an efficient addiction may truthfully say they never feel anything negative.

Secrets and shame

Many people with addictions learn to keep secrets from a very young age though, for many, the secret may be so deeply entrenched that at first it's hard to remember or acknowledge it. The secret may be something as serious as abuse or it might be a parent's alcoholism or infidelity. Or it may be a family secret such as an illegitimate child or domestic violence. Or it may be a more personal secret, such as your own sexuality or your true feelings about going to boarding school or your parents' separation.

Forty-one percent of the survey respondents were aware of secrets in their families (Hall, 2013). In these families there is often an outward projection of order and control and the child learns to keep up the public face of decency and respect and keep quiet about the things that are better left unknown. This sets up a pattern of behaviour in which secrets, double standards or even a double life are the norm.

Shame is another common denominator in the childhoods of people with addiction. Fifty-two percent in the survey said they felt shame in their childhood (Hall, 2013). For some of those, the shame may have been inflicted from outside of the family, perhaps in some form of social discrimination because of sexual or gender diversity, or for racial or religious reasons. For others shame has been used by parents as a tool for control and punishment. Rather than chastising a child when they have done something wrong, they are made to feel bad and worthless as a person. This might be reflected in harsh or critical oral statements or in behaviours such as humiliating punishments or silence.

Both secrets and shame set up the framework for leading a double life and keeping part of yourself hidden from those you love or those who care for you.

Sex education

Understanding why sex, rather than a substance or other behaviour, became the drug of choice is often found within the messages someone learns about sex. Those messages pertain to gender, sexual attitudes and sexual behaviours. Many people with sex addiction were brought up to feel ashamed of their sexuality and therefore find it difficult to express it in a healthy way (41 percent in my survey, Hall, 2013). Sex may have been a taboo subject and masturbation, if acknowledged at all, was either sinful or perverted. Additional negative global messages may have been taught, such as men are dangerous sexual predators, gay men are always promiscuous and women don't like sex, resulting in illicit sexual encounters or paid-for sex. Conversely some are brought up with the belief that sex is a primary need that can be explored and exploited without emotional consideration for self or other. Sex without boundaries is encouraged and normalised.

Whether sex was vilified or glorified, many sex and porn addicts had their first exposure to sexual material from an especially early age (Carnes, 1991, Owens et al., 2012); a surprising 41 percent in my survey said they were using pornography before the age of 12. Of course, many young people grow up today having accessed pornography and not all will develop an addiction. However, I am seeing an increasing number of young men who have never masturbated without pornography and have never considered ever masturbating without it. Pornography used to be a masturbatory accessory, an extra treat, whereas now it is often seen as an essential foundation for it.

Sexual messages and experiences in adolescence can be particularly powerful and long lasting as this is when our sexual templates are becoming cemented in our brains (Money, 1989). Adolescence is also a time when the brain is particularly susceptible to addictions (Gladwin et al., 2011). While most would accept that masturbation is a natural and healthy way of discovering and enjoying one's sexuality, for someone with porn addiction it soon becomes a primary way of coping with the struggles of life. And while most adolescents slowly extend their sexuality towards partners, some lack the courage or the opportunity to do this. Therefore, lone, secretive and often shame-filled sexual behaviours become the norm.

Adolescent loneliness

Adolescence is a time when 'fitting in' with your peers is at its most important. It is a developmental phase where self-identity begins to be laid down and the transition from child to adulthood requires looking more to peers for guidance and affirmation than to parents. Most adolescents will have days when they say they feel like a freak. That might simply be because they don't have the right trainers or haircut, or it may be indicative of a much deeper sense of low self-esteem and separation. For people with sex or porn addiction, there are many more days when it is the latter.

A significant number of addicts report feeling different from their peers. Sixty-four percent in my survey said they often felt left out and different, and one in five cited adolescent loneliness and isolation as the most influential factor in their addiction (Hall, 2013). The isolation may be because of something particular in their family such as following a particular religion or belief system, or it may be because of a difference in perceived social class or intelligence, whether that's struggling with a learning difficulty or being gifted and able. For sexually diverse clients, the isolation may have started in earlier childhood as they began to realise they were different from their peers and led on to an adolescent struggle to understand and accept their own identity. Frequently moving home and changing school is another common factor making it difficult to make relationships that are anything more than transient. Another common factor is shyness – 74 percent described themselves as shy and 43 percent as very shy (Hall, 2013). It's hard to know if some people are born shy or if social difficulties make them shy. Either way, shyness can become a heavy burden that particularly impacts forming healthy relationships and developing support systems. These differences isolate the individual and make it easier to privately seek solace in porn and masturbation. Many clients have reported that while they enjoyed their private life of porn, it created a sense of shame that further alienated them from friends and potential partners. And so the stage is set for addiction.

Mike

Mike's addiction was induced by opportunity. He came to therapy for a pornography addiction which he'd struggled with for the past 12 years – since he was about 15. He spent at least 5 or 6 hours most days looking at online porn. He had always assumed he'd 'grow out of this' when he met the right girl. Three years earlier he had met the right girl and they were now living together. At first the sex was great but gradually he returned to his old habits and now they rarely had sex, which was a major issue for her. Mike was racked with guilt. He loved his girlfriend but she couldn't compete with his online sex life. What's more, he was experiencing more and more frequent episodes of erectile dysfunction and his only recourse was to go back to porn.

As with all addicts, there were multiple contributing factors. Mike was a very a bright child who loved maths, but unfortunately he went to a sporty school. He felt isolated from his peers and was often teased for being a swot. His home was fairly stable. His parents were practising Christians, so rules were quite rigid and sex was never discussed, and with no sisters the opposite sex was a mystery to him.

Mike first saw pornography when he started his secondary education at an all-boys school. Apparently it was part of the unofficial induction. He liked what he saw and being IT-literate he was soon accessing porn on the home computer. His parents assumed he was studying and he knew how to clear the history, so it was easy.

It was hard to pinpoint exactly when Mike became an addict, but he knows his shyness made it difficult for him to connect with others. He described porn as his 'closest and most reliable friend.' He knew some of the other lads from school used online porn too but they also talked about their sexual exploits with girls. He longed for that, but didn't have the courage, so he took further comfort from his secret best friend. It wasn't until he finally met his first and current girlfriend at the age of 24 that he realised how hooked he was.

Trauma-induced addiction

Traumas come in many different shapes and sizes. Some are very obvious, such as violent assaults or childhood abuse, but others are more subtle. Some are one off traumatic events, others are experienced over an extended period of time. For a few, trauma may become a part of everyday life, for example for those who work within the emergency services or armed forces, or to a lesser degree, those who work with the victims of trauma, within the charity sector and psychological services – sometimes referred to as vicarious trauma.

These paragraphs are not intended to tell you everything you need to know about trauma, but rather how it links to addiction. If you have experienced trauma or are working with a client who has, then further reading and study is essential to ensure the trauma can be accessed and worked with in a safe and supportive way.

Abuse

Abuse may be emotional, physical or sexual, and may come from within or outside of the family of origin. When abuse has happened within the family then there will almost definitely be attachment issues as well.

Emotional abuse can be defined as undermining a child's confidence and sense of self-worth, for example by ignoring them, giving degrading punishments, or constantly threatening or humiliating them. When a child is denied the acceptance, love, encouragement, consistency and positive attention they deserve they often grow up thinking they are deficient in some way and not worthy of care or respect. Emotional abuse can also occur at the hands of older siblings, from bullies at school or by teachers or other carers and results in low self-esteem, shame and a reduced ability to healthily care for self or others. Sex with others or masturbation may be used as a way of self-soothing or as a way of self-harming and reinforcing feelings of worthlessness and isolation.

Physical abuse refers to any intentional pain or injury inflicted on another. As with emotional abuse, this may happen at the hands of parents or others in a position of care, or in the form of bullying from peers or within the workplace. On-going physical abuse damages a child's ability to trust others and the energy required to learn about relationships is put into defending against possible risks of harm. Someone who has been physically abused may use sex as a way of forgetting the emotional pain as well as receiving much deserved and needed physical comfort.

Sexual abuse is often one of the hardest areas for someone to identify, especially if it involved minimal or no physical contact, or if the sexual activities were enjoyed. It's important to understand that any behaviour that coerces a child into sexual behaviour, or is instigated by someone in a more powerful position, is abuse. For example, being made to view pornography or watch a sexual act or being used as an object for sexual arousal.

In my survey, 38 percent reported emotional abuse, 17 percent sexual abuse and 16 percent physical abuse (Hall, 2013).

Assault

An assault might best be described as a severe isolated incident of abuse, usually violent, that might be physical or sexual. As with abuse, that may happen within the home but more often it will be an attack by someone outside of the family. In my survey 16 percent had been physically or sexually assaulted. Someone who has survived an assault may use sex not only as a way of managing the emotional impact but also as a way of soothing the physical memories.

Other shocks to the system

We all have to come to terms with losing a loved one at some time in our life, but when it happens prematurely as happened for 21 percent of survey respondents (Hall, 2013), losing a parent, sibling or young partner can be experienced as a trauma.

Sudden illness or disability can also be experienced as a trauma, whether that's to oneself or a loved one. I have had a number of clients who became carers at a young age because of a parent's illness or disability, and this sudden responsibility and subsequent loss of childhood can have similar consequences to experiencing a deliberate act of trauma. Witnessing, or being aware of, domestic violence and abuse is also now commonly accepted as a trauma, something that happened to over one in ten of respondents in my survey (Hall, 2013).

Another type of trauma that I feel is often missed is when a dream or ambition is shattered. On the surface this may seem slight, especially in comparison to abuse, but I have worked with many clients whose behaviour escalated into addiction when their future was suddenly stolen away from them. Examples include; people who always thought they would be a sports professional, but then found out they would never reach the top. Or the academics who shone brightly throughout their schooling years, only to be overtaken at university or in the workplace. The loss of the future they thought was theirs is experienced not just as a bereavement, but also as a loss of identity; who am I now and who will I become? Sudden job loss, whether through redundancy or dismissal, may also be experienced as a trauma, especially when it results in a sudden change of lifestyle.

The impact of trauma

The full impact of trauma can be hard to acknowledge, especially for someone who has successfully used their addiction to soothe their emotional pain. It may also be especially hard for men in our tough-guy culture to admit to themselves, let alone to others, how frightening or upsetting the experiences have been. One writer said that when a sex addict has experienced trauma, especially in childhood, the addiction is not necessarily a pleasure-seeking strategy but a survival strategy (Fisher, 2007). This is because letting go of the addiction may allow the devastating and terrifying feelings of trauma to resurface. Another common scar of trauma is anger. Anger at the aggressor, at the circumstances, at the lack of protection by others, at the inability to defend oneself. Getting lost in a sexual activity can soothe this anger.

Trauma can also influence the choice of sexual behaviours. There has been some evidence that some compulsive fetish behaviours and paraphilias may be linked to previous trauma. 'The Opponent Process Theory of Acquired Motivation' (Soloman, 1980) describes how a negative emotion or experience can be reframed as a positive in order to re-write the script. For example, someone who was bullied and humiliated as a child might pay a dominatrix to sexually arouse them by doing likewise. Hence turning trauma into triumph (Birchard, 2011).

Like sex and porn addiction, our understanding of trauma has changed significantly over the last few years, especially how trauma impacts the brain. It is now known that the imprint of the trauma is in the limbic system and in the brainstem; in other words, it is stored in our primitive animal brains, not in our thinking brain. And the part of the brain known as the amygdala, which is responsible for 'fight and flight,' often remains hypersensitive long after the trauma has passed (Van der Kolk, 1996). This is why someone who's experienced trauma may remain mentally anxious and hypervigilant and have an overactive startle reflex long after any conscious memory of the trauma has passed. This hypersensitive amygdala may be triggered by any number of external sources throwing the body's sympathetic nervous system into what's known as hyperarousal, or the parasympathetic system into hypoarousal, and temporarily by-pass the thinking part of the brain.

Sexual behaviour may become a way for a trauma sufferer to numb feelings of hyperarousal such as hyperactivity, obsessive thinking, rage and panic and also alleviate feelings of disassociation, numbness, depression and exhaustion experienced in hypoarousal. In short, it is thought that addictive behaviours can become an effective technique to regulate the nervous system (Fisher, 2007).

In an on-going online survey at www.sexaddictionhelp.co.uk, 13 percent of the 619 respondents who had completed the OAT questionnaire, described their addiction as purely trauma induced, and 24 percent attachment and trauma induced.

> **Peter**
>
> Peter had a trauma-induced addiction and came for therapy because he was terrified his partner of 10 years was going to find him out. He had a job that meant he was away in Europe 2 or 3 nights a week and whenever he was he would spend hours watching the hotel's pay for TV channels. Over the years he had learned where all the strip clubs, massage parlours and brothels were in most of the major cities around Europe – he joked that he could write a 'rough guide' on the subject.
>
> He described his childhood as difficult but loving. He'd had a sister 5 years younger but she was run over and killed when he was 12. The whole family was obviously badly affected and his parents struggled for a while, but his grandparents were very close and always on hand if his parents weren't. His early teens were marred by the tragedy and he was aware that he never rebelled like some of his friends did. At 15 he started going steady with a girl at school and spent much of his time with her. They got engaged at 24 but at 26, after a few weeks of unexplained illness, she was diagnosed with leukaemia. She died 18 months later.
>
> When I met Peter he was 48, a successful businessman, amicably divorced from his first wife and a father of 3 children. He had first started using porn when he was 26 while his girlfriend was having chemotherapy. He said it helped to take his mind off what she was going through. His addiction had slowly escalated but he'd had many, many months of abstinence at various points in his life. He explained that it had raised its ugly head again 18 months ago when he and his current partner had got engaged. As we worked through his history, he discovered that each time his addiction had returned, it had been when something had unconsciously reminded him of his painful past.

Attachment-induced addiction

Whatever a child experiences in life and whatever opportunities may be presented to them in adolescence, if there is a secure parental attachment they are likely to fare well. Where there is safe, reliable, supportive parenting it's possible for a child to make mistakes, learn from them and move on. It is also easier for them to consciously recover from trauma. But without that fundamental bedrock of what psychologists call 'healthy attachment,' addiction has a greater chance to take root and flourish (Katehakis, 2016).

Healthy attachment starts from the moment we are born. A new-born baby 'attaches' to their primary care giver, usually mum, in order to survive. As the child grows they continue to need that attachment in order to develop healthily. When a child feels nurtured and cared for they have the courage to explore their world, knowing that safety is just a cry away. This attachment is important for emotional as well as physical development. When a child is still in the pre-verbal stage, they need a parent who is empathically attuned to their needs. And as they learn to talk they need a parent who is encouraging and responsive to their efforts to communicate. Without this a child may not develop the necessary skills to recognise and communicate their needs to others appropriately or to recognise and respond to the needs of others – including sexual needs. But the effects are not just emotional, they are also biologically imprinted.

Attachment and the brain

There is growing evidence from neuroscience that insufficient empathic care in early childhood creates a growth-inhibiting environment that produces immature, physiologically undifferentiated orbitofrontal affect regulatory systems (Schore, 2003). In other words, a child whose needs for attention, soothing, stimulation, affection and validation are not met may find the consequences structurally written into their developing brain. The altered prefrontal function is associated with high risk of drug and alcohol addiction (Bechara and Damasio, 2002; Franklin et al., 2002; Goldstein et al., 2001). One proposed explanation for this is that the insecure attachment template is not able to produce its own endogenous opiates and therefore individuals will reach for external opiates to stimulate dopamine reward centres (Hudson Allez, 2009). Additionally, for the insecurely attached individual, the orbitofrontal area of the cortex may no longer producesufficient dopamine or noradrenaline to facilitate sexual excitation and inhibition, and therefore an external source may become increasingly relied upon for something that the brain has not learnt to manufacture for itself.

Parenting styles

There are a number of reasons why attachment may be damaged in childhood, for example from absent, abusive, negligent or inadequate parenting. If a child is physically separated from a parent for adoption or fostering or through bereavement, then there will inevitably be at least a short period of time when good parenting is absent. And abusive parenting, as discussed under trauma, obviously doesn't provide the necessary environment for a child to thrive. Negligent and inadequate parenting are often harder to recognise and some people can understandably get defensive if a therapist is deemed to be blaming a parent who they believe did their best.

Negligent parenting, while not overtly abusive, leaves a child feeling fearful as they are never fully sure how a parent will respond. A negligent parent is inconsistent – caring and attentive one minute and absent, rejecting or cruel the next. Usually this is the result of a parent's own personal problems, and they may be aware of their inadequacies and be apologetic to the child. The term 'inadequate parenting' can be used to describe the childhood situation where parents were unavailable or unresponsive due to extenuating circumstances – for example, physical or emotional illness of themselves or another child, parental separation or divorce, victim of domestic violence, extreme poverty or simply because of naivety. It's important with both of these parenting situations not to blame the parents but to recognise that the consequences may have been a contributing factor to how the addiction got started.

Finally there are many whose childhoods were disrupted by long periods of separation from home, often in the guise of being a benefit, rather than a wound. 11 percent of people with sex addiction went to boarding school (Hall, 2013). Whilst some may experience no negative consequences from their schooling, others felt abandoned and/or terrified. For all, a template is established for living two separate lives, one at home, one away and this split may continue into adult life as acting out behaviours are easily compartmentalised into 'another' life.

There are many different degrees of unhealthy attachment. Some people may always have known that their problems result from poor parenting and their addiction is primarily caused by these wounds, whereas others see it as a minor contributing factor. In an on-going online survey at www.sexaddictionhelp.co.uk, 32 percent of the 619 respondents who had completed the OAT questionnaire, described their addiction as attachment induced, and a further 24 percent described it as attachment and trauma induced.

> **Bill**
>
> Bill had an attachment-induced addiction. He came for therapy aged 42 having been to many other therapists for his problem. He had been married for 18 years, had 2 children and his wife had always known about his sex addiction and supported him in finding help. The problem was she didn't truly know its full extent. Bill had managed to keep hidden how often he acted out and the massive debt he'd run up as a consequence. Bill had first used prostitutes in his early 20s when he was working on a construction project in Soho. He described how everyone used prostitutes there; it was normal. Since then he had developed a penchant for the best, most expensive woman he could buy. 'It's my treat,' he explained.
>
> Bill had an impoverished childhood. He had never known his dad and his mum brought him up alone in a high rise flat on benefits. He was an only child and spent most of his growing up trying to look after his mum. She struggled with depression and was reliant on major tranquilisers for most of his childhood. Bill learned to cook and clean from an early age and he never asked for anything for himself – that would not have been fair. He was ashamed to admit that he was embarrassed by his home and his mum, and on the rare occasions he went to a friend's house, he was consumed with envy. Life was unfair.
>
> Bill loved his wife and he cared for her, but through his addiction, he ensured he had another outlet where his needs could be reliably met.

References

Bechara, A., & Damasio, H. (2002) Decision-making and addiction (part 1): Impaired motivation of somatic states in substance dependent individuals when pondering decisions with negative future consequences, *Neuropsychologia*, 40: 1675–1689.

Birchard, T. (2011) Sexual Addiction and the Paraphilias, *Sexual Addiction & Compulsivity*, 18: 3.

Carnes, P. (1991) *Don't call it love: Recovery from sexual addiction*, Bantam, New York.

Fisher, J. (2007) *Addictions and Trauma Recovery*, Basic Books, New York.

Franklin, T.R., Acton, P.D., Maldjian, J.A., Gray, J.D., Croft, J.R., Dackis, C.A., O'Brien, C.P., & Childress, A.R. (2002) Decreased Gray Mater Concentration in Insular, Orbitofrontal, Cingulate, and Temporal Cortices of Cocaine Patients, *Biological Psychiatry*, 51: 134–143.

Gladwin, T.E., Figner, B., Crone, E.A. & Wiers, R.W. (2011) Addiction, adolescence and the integration of control and motivation, *Developmental Cognitive Neuroscience*, 1(4): 364–376.

Goldstein, R.Z., Volkow, N.D., Wang, G.J., Fowler, J.S., & Rajaram, S. (2001) Addiction changes in orbitofrontal gyrus function: involvement in response inhibition, *Neuroreport 8*, 12(11): 2595–2599.

Hall, P. (2013) *Understanding and Treating Sex Addiction*, Routledge, London.

Hall, P. (2017) *A Biopsychosocial View of Sex Addiction, International Handbook of Sexual Addiction*, Routledge, London.

Hudson-Allez, G. (2009) *Infant Searches, Adult Losses*, Routledge, London.

Katehakis, A. (2016) *Sex Addiction as Affect Dysregulation: A Neurobiologically Informed Holistic Treatment*, W.W. Norton, New York.

Money, J. (1989) *Vandalised Love Maps*, Prometheus Books, Buffalo NY.

Owens, E., Behin, R., Manning, J., & Reid, R. (2012) The impact of internet pornography on adolescents: a review of the research, *Sexual Addiction & Compulsivity*, 19(1–2): 99–122.

Schore, A.N. (2003) *Affect Regulation and Disorders of the Self*, W.W. Norton, New York.

Soloman, R. (1980) The Opponent process theory of acquired motivation. The costs of pleasure and the benefits of pain, *American Psychologist*, 35(8): 691–712.

Van der Kolk, B. (1996) *Traumatic Stress*, The Guilford Press, New York.

4 How addiction is maintained and reinforced

All of us will at some stage in our life, be attracted to an addictive substance or behaviour. That may be drugs, alcohol, food, gambling or perhaps exercise or work. But most of us are able to pull back. We recognise within us a point where our indulgence is becoming problematic and we either curtail our habit or stop all together. We know that although we may be enjoying what we're doing, it's either already beginning to harm us or will do at some point in the future.

There are a number of reasons why this doesn't happen for people with an addiction. And like causes, these maintaining factors can be viewed through the BERSC model (Hall, 2013). As highlighted in the previous chapter, in part this is because of biological factors such as brain chemistry. The more someone uses a chemical or behaviour to produce a dopamine high, the less able the brain is to produce sufficient through its own resources. And the more effective the high, the stronger the memory and the brain's orientation towards seeking it again. For a trauma survivor, the brain has become hypersensitive to arousal and therefore more vulnerable to seeking external opioids for self-soothing.

There are also significant emotional, relational, societal and cultural influences that both maintain and reinforce the addictive behaviour. It is perhaps more important to understand these maintaining factors than it is to know what caused the addiction, since it is in breaking these patterns that recovery is found. In the same way as every person with an addiction has a unique history that has led them to addiction, so each will also have a unique combination of factors that reinforce and maintain it.

In this chapter we will explore those influences as they relate to opportunity-induced, trauma-induced and attachment-induced addiction but first it's important to recognise and understand that all addictions operate within a cycle. A cycle that, if not recognised, can keep someone unknowingly, and indefinitely, trapped.

The cycles of addiction

There are many different cycles of addiction that have been offered over the years that can help us to understand why it's so difficult to break out of addiction. Here I would like to offer two – each of which demonstrates a different dimension of the addictive process.

Oscillating release/control cycle

The idea of this figure-of-eight model, which continually flows between *control* and *release*, was first offered by Fossum and Mason in 1986, (see Figure 4.1). Since then it has been adapted by a number of addiction professionals to explain how someone can swing between states of mind and behaviours that are rigid and controlled to release behaviours that may be experienced as either euphoric or despairing.

As you can see from Figure 4.1, there are many activities that can be classed as either *control* or *release* and, for people with an addiction, both are equally damaging, as they will eventually lead to the other side of the cycle. For example, although porn avoidance accompanied by a harsh regime of work and exercise may at first seem like a sensible and healthy alternative to porn addiction, in reality it will only be a matter of time before someone becomes exhausted and disheartened, and slips back into the *release* side of the cycle. The *release* behaviours are temporarily experienced as a welcome break from the *control*, but as guilt and shame and other negative consequences gradually creep in, so you're then thrown back into the *control* side of the cycle again.

This control/release cycle can also describe the person who finds their only escape from a high-stress job is engaging in an equally stress inducing and compulsive behaviour. For example, those in the armed forces or emergency and medical services, who must remain

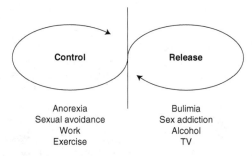

Figure 4.1 Oscillating release/control cycle

hypervigilant throughout the work day but then let off steam through binge porn use. Or those in the financial or legal services who often work exhausting hours, whilst managing enormous responsibility and find respite in stimulant drugs and sex parties. For some, reducing their work load is essential to combat the inevitable need for release, whereas for others, alternative ways of finding relaxation are required.

The six-phase cycle

The six-phase cycle shown in Figure 4.2 is the cycle that I have developed over the years of my practice to help clients recognise how their addiction continues to maintain itself through their behaviours, thoughts and emotions (Hall, 2013). This is a cycle that is now widely used by many sex addiction therapists around the world. The length of each phase, and the length of time between each phase, varies from individual to individual, as does the content.

The shape of the model is also relevant as it demonstrates how intensity gradually builds from the *dormant* phase until a *trigger* speeds the build-up through the *preparation* phrase. The height of the cycle is *acting out* but this quickly drops to *regret* and *reconstitution* before gradually returning to *dormant*. However, this should not necessarily be confused with the 'high point' of the cycle as many people with addiction, as explored in Chapter 1, do not enjoy their behaviour and often describe themselves as 'acting out' purely to end the craving and enable themselves to get into reconstitution. We will explore each of the six phases as they relate to opportunity-induced, trauma-induced and attachment-induced addiction in depth over the coming pages, but, in brief, they can be summarised as below.

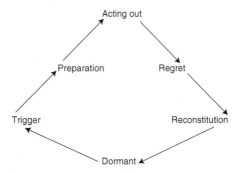

Figure 4.2 The six-phase cycle of addiction

1   *Dormant* – the phase where the addiction is temporarily in remission but underlying issues remain unresolved. Life may appear 'normal,' but it's only a matter of time before a trigger occurs.
2   *Trigger* – the trigger is an event, an opportunity, a bodily sensation, emotion or thought process that activates the behaviour. There may be a single trigger, but often they are multiple and may be conscious or unconscious.
3   *Preparation* – the preparation phase can vary in length considerably from just a few minutes to open a web page, to many weeks of planning an affair. It includes practical preparations and psychological strategies.
4   *Acting out* – for some, acting out is a single event such as visiting a sex worker, which may last just a few minutes, whereas for others it may be a week-long binge of pornography use.
5   *Regret* – depending on the consequences of acting out, the regret phase may be experienced as little more than a momentary 'ooops' or weeks of despair, shame and self-loathing.
6   *Reconstitution* – this is where life is either consciously or unconsciously put back together again, including rebuilding self-esteem, covering tracks and/or renewing resolutions not to act out again.

The dormant phase

The dormant phase is perhaps the hardest for anyone to recognise, especially for those who may stay dormant for weeks, months or even years at a time. Typically, a porn addiction may only be dormant for a relatively brief amount of time as there is ample opportunity to trigger the addictive behaviours, whereas other addictions may be dormant for much longer. During this dormant phase most people will be functioning perfectly adequately although some may have switched their addiction to something else. Some will use alcohol, work or exercise as an alternative way of self-soothing during this phase, or distracting themselves from withdrawal. But where no other addiction is used, it's tempting to assume that the addiction is under control or has gone away all together. What's important to recognise is that if the underlying causes of addiction have not been identified and resolved, the proverbial sword of Damocles is still hanging overhead. Dormancy is not the same as recovery.

For everyone, the opportunity-induced causes, such as difficulties with self-control and emotional regulation, are still present, as is a behavioural pattern of having secrets and living a double life. In addition, many may continue to be working in a highly sexualised environment or have regular and easy access to porn or sex workers.

For those with a trauma-induced addiction there will still be the scars of previous abuse or assault causing difficulties in regulating hyper and hypo arousal states. While nothing in the dormant phase is activating these states, a period of relative calm can be enjoyed. However, unless healthy strategies are learnt and adopted, the vulnerability to triggers continues to be high.

Attachment-induced addiction may stay dormant for an extended period of time, especially if a new relationship is found that can temporarily relieve feelings of loneliness and fears of rejection. It's common for an attachment-induced addict to feel that the new relationship has solved their problems, but the inevitable difficulties that arise in any relationship are likely to tip the balance at some point in the future.

The triggers

The dormant phase of the addiction cycle will, in time, be interrupted by a trigger or series of triggers. For some people, triggers come out of the blue but for others there is either a conscious or unconscious building of tension, and the final trigger may be awaited or even sought out.

For those with a pure opportunity-induced addiction, the trigger will almost always be an event or circumstance that creates the opportunity to act out. That might be an empty house or easy internet access. Or it could be working at home for the day or a business meeting that will provide an easy opportunity to visit a sex worker or hook up with a stranger online. If multiple affairs are the drug of choice it might be a new person starting at the office or a business conference with an attractive colleague.

These opportunity triggers will be equally powerful for all categories of addiction, but they are often accompanied by a negative emotional state. For someone with a trauma-induced addiction, emotional or physical feelings of anxiety or numbness can trigger a desire to self soothe. Whereas, for people with an attachment-induced addiction there are more likely to be feelings of loneliness, isolation, rejection or suffocation that require soothing.

Sexual desire may also be a trigger for each classification of addiction, though as discussed in Chapter 1, this will rarely have its roots in libido and, particularly for those with an attachment induced addiction, it is more commonly linked to a desire for intimacy and affirmation than sexual release.

The preparation phase

Once triggered, the addiction enters the preparation phase of the cycle and the necessary practical and psychological arrangements are made to act out. This preparation stage is as much part of the addiction as the acting out phase. While in this place the trauma- and attachment-induced addictions are already escaping their emotional pain and all are increasing their arousal and anticipation. I have had clients who have spent months preparing themselves for the next time they'll meet someone for sex. They have spent hours every day on meticulous research and planning, scouring hook up apps or dating sites or looking at sex worker profiles. This phase is often described as being the most enjoyable. As explained in Chapter 1, sex addiction often has very little to do with sex.

Whatever type of addiction, most people will make at least some rudimentary plans to ensure they can act out without being caught. That might include; changing their schedules or travel arrangements, creating an alibi for being online, such as checking emails or studying, or being away from home, creating private email accounts and bank accounts, or any number of other things. Some people are not consciously aware of the preparations they are making because they are so caught up in the emotional bubble that it creates, or stuck in denial. This is a common phenomenon in addictions and is often referred to as S.U.D.s – Seemingly Unimportant Decisions. An example of an S.U.D. would be when someone says they 'just happened to be in Soho,' without acknowledging that the business meeting was arranged weeks before, as was the hotel room and just enough untraceable cash to pay a sex worker.

The psychological strategies engaged during the preparation phase can be described in two ways; cognitive distortions and limiting core beliefs. We will look now at each of these in turn.

COGNITIVE DISTORTIONS

All of us experience cognitive distortions and will at times use them to our advantage. By consciously, or unconsciously, thinking in a certain way, we can change how we feel about something and consequently change how we behave. It's a common strategy we all employ when we want to do something that we really know we shouldn't. For example, imagine it's late at night, it's raining and you desperately need milk. You drive to a local shop where you find parking restrictions outside and nowhere else to park. Now look at Table 4.1, which lists common cognitive distortions and see how they can be used to help you park illegally.

Table 4.1 Common cognitive distortions

Rationalisation	If it was daytime I wouldn't park here, but it's late at night so I won't be causing an obstruction
Justification	It's raining and I don't have an umbrella
Minimisation	I'm only going to be two minutes
Magnification	The only other place to park is absolutely miles away and it will take forever to walk from there
Blame	If my partner had remembered the milk I wouldn't be in this position
Entitlement	I've had a really hard day today, it wouldn't be fair to expect me to walk further than I have to
Uniqueness	It's ok for me to park here because I've lived here for over 20 years and I've always been very generous to the community
Mental filter	I'm not going to let myself remember the parking ticket I got last week
Normalisation	Everyone parks on double yellow lines in this situation
Invincibility	I won't get caught – I never get caught

As you can see, there are many, many different ways to create the environment where we allow ourselves to do something that we don't think is right. Many people with addiction describe it as having two voices in their head. Or the devil on one shoulder and an angel on the other. One voice is saying 'Don't do it' but the other is constantly feeding messages that distort thinking until the first voice gives up.

Acting out

As explained in Chapter 1, all addictions serve a function – a function that is above and beyond pure sexual pleasure and fulfilment. That's not to deny the fact that most people enjoy what they do, at least at first, but to understand why they continue to return to a behaviour that causes so much destruction in their lives, you need to understand the deeper need that it fulfils.

In a nutshell, all addiction is used to manage emotional pain. At the simplest level, it soothes the pain of not acting out, by ending the craving and preoccupation. Many people with addiction also report using sex or porn to manage anger and frustration, to relieve boredom, stress and anxiety, and to alleviate loneliness and feelings of low self-esteem. To an outsider, these may appear to be poor excuses for acting out, but it's important to remember that most addicts have few or no other coping mechanisms. What's more, for those with a trauma-induced and/or an attachment-induced addiction, the feelings can be overwhelming.

Someone with a trauma-induced addiction may be using acting out as a way of regulating hyper- and hypo-arousal states (Fisher, 2007). As you can see from Figure 4.3, the hyper-arousal state is when our bodies are thrown into fight or flight; hypo arousal is when we are thrown into freeze. Both of these extremes are physically, emotionally and psychologically painful, and addiction can be used to alleviate the symptoms and bring the central nervous system back to its normal state. We may all experience these hyper- and hypo-arousal states at some time in our lives but, for a trauma sufferer, the window of tolerance is narrower and therefore they can be thrown into one of these states quickly and easily.

For someone with an attachment-induced addiction, the acting-out phase of the cycle will primarily be used to soothe relational pain. For example, to soothe loneliness and to receive affection and attention, or they may use the behaviour as an intimacy regulator to stop themselves getting too emotionally involved with one partner who might suffocate or abandon them.

For people with either attachment induced and/or trauma induced addiction there is also another somewhat contrary benefit they may

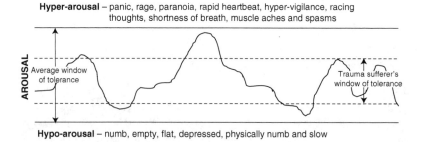

Figure 4.3 The window of tolerance
Source: Adapted with kind permission from Ogden, Minton and Pain, 2006

get from acting out, especially when their behaviour involves risk. People with a history of either trauma or disrupted attachment often struggle with extreme fear, whether that's fear of being relationally or physically hurt. When taking risks, we overcome that fear. On the surface we may think that risk-taking behaviours demonstrate a lack of fear, but often, unconsciously, they are a way of proving to ourselves that we can survive it – by creating fear and beating it.

Achieving the required function may take minutes or days and it's important to remember part of this function will already be starting during the preparation phase. One person may achieve their need for affection or escape hyper arousal in a brief period of time, but others may need to binge on their chosen behaviour in order to gain the required result. Whatever the function, once achieved the addiction then enters the regret phase.

The regret phase

Some people with addiction immediately identify with the regret phase, whereas others say they feel little or no remorse. The reaction depends on two things: first, the negative consequences experienced; and second the amount of cognitive distortions employed to reduce those consequences. For example, if someone is instantly faced with financial loss, contracting or transmitting an STI, or an angry partner, they will feel more regret than someone who has 'got away with it' unscathed. And someone who feels great shame at their pornography use, or has made promises to accountability partners will feel more self-loathing because it violates their personally held values.Shame is by far the most common, and perhaps most devastating, consequence of sexual addiction, as we will explore further in Chapter 10. The shame may be the result of the actual behaviour contravening strongly held beliefs and values, such as not exploiting vulnerable people such as sex workers who may have been forced into the trade. Or it may be at living a double life and lying to loved ones. Or the shame may be a result of being too weak to break the cycle of addiction and having failed to live up to one's own intentions and expectations.

The regret phase can last for just a few minutes for some, to weeks and months for others. If the behaviour seriously contradicts someone's beliefs and values, then the resulting shame and damage to self-esteem can be immense to the point where the reconstitution stage is almost impossible and the shame becomes the trigger to act out again. Some people with a trauma-induced addiction can become so worried about the possible consequences of being discovered that they create their own trauma that can trip them into hyper or hypo arousal states. For most, the regret phase is the most painful place in the cycle and some will have better resources than others to get themselves into reconstitution.

Reconstitution

Reconstitution is the phase where life is put back together again. What that means will depend on how much life has fallen apart during acting out. Some people with online addictions who binge spend the reconstitution phase looking after their physical needs. They may not have eaten, washed or slept properly for days, so this will be their first priority. Those who visit sex workers might be getting a health check at the GUM clinic, looking at how to replenish their finances and ensuring there is no traceable evidence for a partner or work colleague to discover. If the reconstitution phase is accompanied by a commitment to 'never act out again,' then hard drives may be deleted, porn blockers reinstalled, email accounts cancelled and future business trips changed.

For those whose addiction affects their educational, work or social life, extra hours may be put in to make up for what's been lost. Partners often unknowingly benefit during this stage as more effort is put into relationships, perhaps with thoughtful gifts and caring gestures that, to the unknowing partner, seem to come out of the blue or perhaps are seen as a welcome sign of reconciliation after an unexplained time of emotional distance.

Putting self-esteem back together can be a much tougher job than managing the practicalities. Cognitive distortions can help to minimise, normalise or excuse the behaviour, but most still find themselves battling with depression and anxiety until they can get themselves back on their feet again. Some may resort to another addiction such as alcohol, drugs or excessive work or exercise to take their mind off the pain of what they've done. Others go into therapy but never confess the true reason for their distress. In time, for some, days, for others, months, life does go back to normal again. But it's the false 'pretend normal' of the dormant phase, where the underlying issues remain unresolved and often unacknowledged, and the same vulnerability remains, waiting for the next trigger.

Tim

Tim came for therapy very aware of his addictive cycle though he didn't call it that. 'I'm trapped on the same old merry go round,' he explained. 'Over and over and over again, I do the same old thing. It's driving me crazy.'

Tim's addiction was to cyber chat and it was attachment-induced. He came from a very strict family where he was not allowed to mix with other children and he was constantly criticised for not being academically bright enough. He described his childhood as lonely and harsh. He could remain in the dormant phase of the cycle for many weeks but would inevitably be triggered whenever he had an argument with his wife. At first he claimed that she always started the rows, but on reflection he acknowledged that there were some occasions when he deliberately provoked her.

The arguments, which often lasted for days, consisted of his wife criticising him for his inadequacies and insisting that he sleep in the spare room – where they kept the PC. Although he hated the arguments, this fuelled his cognitive distortions during the preparation phase. He felt justified in blaming her for his online diversions and would tell himself that he deserved a little TLC for putting up with her unreasonable tirades. While acting out he felt appreciated and valued by his online sexual companions, but when his wife finally apologised, which she always did after a day or two, he would feel guilty and ashamed of what he'd done. He would try to tell himself that no real harm was done, but he knew his secret online lovers made it much harder to make love to his wife, something she was always desperate to do in order to make up.

During the reconstitution phase, Tim would delete the history on the PC and delete all the contacts in his secret email account. He would throw himself into the relationship, promising his wife that he would be less irritating and promising himself that he would be more tolerant of the exacting standards that she imposed on him. Tim's guilt and shame prevented him from fully confronting his wife about their ongoing relationship issues, and he never considered alternative strategies for if it happened again. And it always did.

References

Fisher, J. (2007) *Addictions and Trauma Recovery*, Basic Books, New York.
Fossum, Merle A., & Mason, Marilyn J. (1986) *Facing Shame: Families in Recovery*, W.W. Norton, New York.
Hall, P. (2013) *Understanding and Treating Sex Addiction*, Routledge, London.
Ogden, P., Minton, K., & Pain, C. (2006) *Trauma and the Body: A Sensorimotor Approach to Psychotherapy*, W.W. Norton, New York.

5 The impact on partners and relationships

Partners are often the forgotten victims of sex and porn addiction. Most knew nothing about their partner's behaviour until discovery day and the news is devastating. A few may have known about occasional pornography use or may have known of an affair, but the extent of acting out is almost always a complete shock. The impact on a relationship is obviously devastating. Trust is obliterated in a second and may take many, many years to restore. The person with the addiction has to get into recovery while the partner finds support to come to terms with the roller coaster of emotions they feel. The couple relationship may not survive, or may not feel worth salvaging. Either way most couples need help with communication during the turbulent time before a decision is made, especially if they have children.

There is not space in this book to discuss all the issues that arise for partners or the impact on relationships. You'll find much more in my other books, Sex Addiction – The Partner's Perspective (Hall, 2016), and the soon to be released, Sex Addiction – A Guide for Couples. What's offered here is an overview of how sex and porn addiction most commonly affects partners and couple relationships and how these issues impact on the recovery of the addict.

The impact on partners

When sex addiction is either revealed or discovered the impact is twofold. Not only is there an intense feeling of betrayal, similar to that experienced with infidelity, but also there is the alarm of discovering a partner is an addict. In addition, some partners are also confronted with sexual behaviours or porn genres that may cause them disbelief, confusion and perhaps disgust. Beneath the intense shock, there are other emotions that compete for dominance in the days and weeks that follow discovery. Some common emotional reactions are listed below.

Shock	Denial	Anger
Confusion	Isolation	Shame
Betrayal	Despair	Doubt
Fear	Sadness	Guilt
Disgust	Disbelief	Hopelessness
Grief	Depression	Numbness
Anxiety	Relief	Foolishness

Partners often describe themselves as being on an emotional rollercoaster, not knowing which way is up and struggling to believe what's happening to them. The partner who has most often been loved, trusted and respected for many years is no longer the person they thought they knew. This leaves them questioning not only their partner, but also themselves. Am I a good judge of character? Am I able to recognise fact from fiction? Can I trust my thoughts and feelings? Who is my partner? What kind of world do I live in?

In reality, their partner is still the same person they always were and there is no reason to doubt most of the qualities they'd enjoyed in their relationship. But now there is a critical extra piece of information. Information that will change both the partner and the future of the relationship forever.

The cultural context of those within GSRD (gender, sexual and relationship diversity) communities can make the revelation of sex or porn addiction especially confusing. If the relationship had been an open one, then deciding which boundaries have been crossed and where trust has been broken may be harder to establish. For some it is also more difficult to find support and empathy from within a community that accepts sexual diversity and may not understand the complexities of addiction.

For male partners in heterosexual relationships there are also additional complications. As we explore further in Chapter 6, female sex and porn addiction is shrouded in even greater secrecy and shame than male addiction and women who betray often come under greater societal attack. These differences impact male partners and often leave them even more isolated than their female counterparts and struggling with greater deterioration of their self-confidence and self-esteem.

The BERSC model (Hall, 2013), discussed earlier in this book is a helpful lens for working with partners too, to ensure that individual needs and social contexts are understood and worked with.

The impact of disclosure

Evidence shows (Schneider et al., 1998) that disclosure of sex addiction is rarely a one-off event. Most often a partner will receive a gradual disclosure as more and more behaviour is either revealed or discovered. While it's easy to assume that this pattern of disclosure is a result of denial and dishonesty on the side of the addict, it is often more linked to a desire to protect the partner from being overwhelmed or making an irrevocable decision to end the relationship. When disclosure, or discovery is gradual, it leaves partners experiencing multiple betrayals and worrying that they may never know the truth.

It is common for partners to endlessly interrogate and seek more and more information and details, a process that is exhausting for both, partly as a way of ensuring everything is out in the open, but also in an unconscious attempt to feel a sense of control. Some feel that once they have all the facts, they'll know what they're facing and can make a decision about the future. In part this is true, but as many can testify, there are some things that are best left unknown. Particularly if it's information that leaves a visual image in the brain, such as looking at porn images or asking questions about sexual acts and people that then imprint themselves into the brain. Once an image is inside the brain it is very difficult to get out (as many addicts know for themselves) and in reality, these details are generally unnecessary and can cause more psychological harm for the partner (Hall, 2016).

Recovery for partners

As stated at the beginning of this chapter, unfortunately there is not room in this book to fully explore the needs of partners who find themselves the innocent victims of sex or porn addiction. Needless to say, those needs are extensive and important and partners must be allowed space to share their feelings openly, knowing they won't be judged and trusting they'll receive the empathy, care and support they deserve. Full details about the recovery process for partners is explained in Sex Addiction – The Partner's Perspective (Hall, 2016), but in brief, recovery means learning to SURF. The acrostic SURF comes from the well-known saying by mindfulness guru, Jon Kabat-Zinn 'You can't stop the waves, but you can learn to surf.'

SURF can be a useful acrostic to remember the key stages of recovery for partners:-

S – *Survive the trauma*

However the addiction is discovered, when reality hits, shock follows. And as the numbness of shock fades, most partners experience a flood of overwhelming emotions. The emotional rollercoaster usually runs for at least six months and the most all partners can hope for is simply to survive. Therapy needs to focus on managing these emotions and discouraging knee jerk decisions, whilst being mindful of both mental and sexual health concerns.

U – *Understand the cycle of reaction*

Like the cycle of addiction, many partners find themselves trapped in a cycle of reaction (Hall, 2016). One minute they feel as though they can cope and are beginning to make sense of what's happened and get themselves back together again – then bang – they're back to square one again. This cycle is explored in depth in my partner book, but in brief, like people with an addiction, partners need to learn to recognise and manage triggers, overcome self-limiting beliefs, self-soothe in a healthy way and resolve any historic issues that might be contributing to their struggle to cope.

R – *Repair self identity and self esteem*

Perhaps the most damaging impact of sex and porn addiction is what it does to a partner's self esteem. Most partners wrestle with self-doubt for years after discovering addiction, even those who logically know it's not their fault. Whether a partner chooses to stay or leave the relationship, many need therapeutic help to rebuild their sense of personal identity and self-worth.

F – *Face the future*

The future for partners is always changed by addiction, not just in terms of the future of the relationship, but also the impact on family members, friendships and lifestyle. Helping a partner to recognise that they continue to have choices and can rebuild a life that is meaningful and rewarding is a key intervention for long-term recovery.

I am absolutely delighted that over the six years since writing the first edition of this book, the automatic labelling of co-dependent on partners of sex and porn addiction has mostly disappeared and instead a relational trauma model has taken its place. But for those more familiar with working with chemical addiction, this mistake is still often made which can add insult to injury for partners. It is widely recognised now that most partners are completely unaware of the addiction and the familiar traits of co-dependency, like preoccupation with their partners' behaviours, obsessive checking and difficulties in their own day to day functioning are common in people who have experienced a traumatic betrayal (Steffens and Means, 2009).

There are undoubtedly some situations where partners are collusive in the behaviour and this seems to be particularly apparent in partners of those with an attachment induced sex or porn addiction. In these cases, the couple relationship has often been impaired by attachment difficulties over many years and the original unconscious fit may have supported the addiction. As with addicts, all partners are different. And all couple relationships are different.

The impact on couple relationships

Having worked as a couple counsellor for nearly 25 years, I can honestly say that nothing impacts a couple relationship in such a devastating way as sex and porn addiction. The impact on each member of the couple is unique. The partner, as we've seen, is traumatised and reeling with shock and betrayal, the person with the addiction is living their worst nightmare; facing the reality of possibly losing everything they have, whilst giving up their only coping mechanism. Both feel exposed, vulnerable and bewildered and almost certainly further apart from each other than they ever could have imagined.

There are two main reasons why sex and porn addiction hurts couple relationships so much. First, it wrecks trust and second, it damages intimacy.

How addiction wrecks trust

Healthy relationships are built on trust. Trusting that the other keeps their commitments, large and small. That they'll always have your best interests at heart and will stand by you in good times and bad.

The impact on a partner's trust is obvious. They discover that the person they've committed their life to has been leading a double life.

They have lied, deceived, cheated and manipulated the other into believing, either that their relationship was safe and sound, or that any problems they faced were caused by something else, perhaps even the partner themselves. Of course not all relationship difficulties will be caused by the undisclosed addiction, but the addiction will almost certainly have exacerbated them and prevented them from being addressed appropriately. But sex and porn addiction damages an addict's trust too. The addict may have spent years living in doubt about the love within their relationship. Doubting their own feelings towards their partner and questioning 'how could I do this if I truly loved them.' They also doubt their partner's love for them, knowing that their partner doesn't truly know them and perhaps would never have chosen to be with them if they had.

The impact on intimacy

Sex and porn addiction damages intimacy within couple relationships, not just when it's discovered, but over the years of active addiction that precede disclosure. Trust is of course, the bedrock of intimacy, it's what allows us to feel safe with others and be open about ourselves, but when a relationship has been overshadowed by sex or porn addiction, knowingly or unknowingly, intimacy will be affected.

That doesn't mean that there will have been no intimacy at all, but the secrecy and shame of sex and porn addiction inevitably erodes intimacy for most couples. As the addictive behaviours escalate, either by spending more and more time online viewing porn or going offline into live sexual encounters, there is less and less energy for the relationship. The person with the addiction often withdraws from emotional communication as their guilt and shame grow. Partners usually sense this withdrawal, and without an explanation, may find themselves either getting into increasing conflict over the lack of intimacy or withdrawing from the relationship themselves for protection.

Sexual intimacy is also impacted for most couples. Some addicts completely withdraw from any kind of sexual relationship, whilst some never fully engaged from the start. Others withdraw more gradually, either by wanting less and less sexual contact, or being less present during sex, or struggling with sexual dysfunctions such as lowered libido, difficulty getting aroused or experiencing orgasm. Many addicts describe how high levels of porn use have changed their sexual tastes and subsequently they feel less and less sexually fulfilled with their partners. Some partners report feeling pressured to go beyond their sexual comfort zones or noticing that their partner always seemed distracted during sex.

Sex addiction is not like any other addiction because it damages the very core of our humanity – our relationships. Sexual identities are left in tatters, with partners often feeling they have been sexually abused by the deceit and betrayal – and addicts feeling like the perpetrators of that abuse.

Recovery for couples

As we've seen, sex and porn addiction is still widely misunderstood and shrouded in secrecy and shame, leaving couples unsure where to turn for help and support. Regrettably there also continues to be a woeful lack of professional help, meaning couples who turn to relationship counsellors, untrained in the area of addiction, may fail to understand the unique difficulties and be unable to illicit change. And those who go for professional help as individuals may find they are receiving different information and advice, which can inevitably lead to further conflict within the couple relationship.

The most important thing couples need to recover from addiction is time – and regrettably that is often something that neither wants to commit to. Once the person with the addiction is in recovery, they are often impatient for their partner to leave the past behind and move on. And partners are understandably often impatient to make a decision about the future of the relationship, though the first six months, whilst the trauma is still being worked through, is usually the worse time to make such a life-changing decision – especially if children are involved. In my book, Sex Addiction – A Guide for Couples (forthcoming), the metaphor of a boat in a storm is used to explain the process of recovery. The boat represents the relationship and the discovery of sex or porn addiction is the tidal wave that capsizes the boat. The couples are crew members, each responsible for their individual survival and the decision whether to rescue the boat or not. Those who choose to stay together will need to develop the tools to rebuild their boat, or perhaps fashion a new one, better equipped for the journey ahead. Those who separate need to ensure they don't go down with the ship and steer towards other shores, mindful of any other crew members on board, such as children. The boat metaphor is a powerful way of helping couples to reflect individually and jointly on the quality of their relationship, their roles as partners and the direction they wish their lives to go. There is more on relationships in Chapter 14.

How partner reactions and relationship issues affect addiction recovery

There is no doubt that the loving support of a partner significantly increases the likelihood of recovery from sex and porn addiction. This is further assisted if the couple are able to work together to strengthen their commitment and intimacy and fight the addiction side by side. However, this is often far too much to expect from a partner who has not only been betrayed and deceived, but who might rightly claim that if they'd known the truth about their partner, they may never have loved them in the first place.

When a partner stays in shame and blame the cycle of addiction may continue as the addict is continually reminded of the pain they have caused. Similarly, if a partner is not able to find the necessary resources to cope for themselves, the addict is likely to put more energy into their partner's recovery than into their own. There are some partners who seem to successfully take control of the situation and will endeavour to help in the recovery process, but where this involves infantilising and/or controlling the addict, their partner may never develop their own internal locus of control and establish their own coping strategies. If a partner leaves, this can devastate the addict to the point where recovery seems pointless since they have already lost what was most important to them. Or it magnifies the trauma or attachment issues that are at the root of the addiction. Conversely, some addicts know that their relationship has been dysfunctional, but rather than addressing this, they have allowed it to be a reason for their addictive behaviours. But in the wake of the discovery of addiction, they feel increasingly duty bound to work at the relationship.

When recovering from sex addiction, having a fulfilling and stable couple relationship can be both a support and an incentive. For many people, a happy couple relationship is one of the most important things in their lives. A place where they can love and be loved. Where they can find peace, comfort and support as well as stimulation and pleasure. A place that provides a refuge from the struggles of life. Therefore, it's perhaps not surprising that the quality of the couple relationship is a key influencer of successful lifelong recovery. When a relationship is not happy, as most aren't after the discovery of addiction, a huge strain can be put on every area of life. This is especially true when there is pain, conflict or threats of separation – all of which are commonplace after the disclosure of sex addiction. Improving couple relationships needs to be a key focus for relapse prevention, since failure to do so may continue to trigger the addict in a myriad of ways.

When an addict is in a relationship, the impact on the partner and how they work through it, either together or apart, significantly affects the treatment process. Wherever possible, services need to be provided for the person with the addiction, the partner and the couple relationship so each can recover and rebuild their lives.

References

Hall, P. (2013) *Understanding and Treating Sex Addiction*, Routledge, London.

Hall, P. (2016) *Sex Addiction: The Partner's Perspective*, Routledge, London.

Schneider, J.P., Corley, D. & Irons, R. (1998) Surviving Disclosure of Infidelity: Results of an International Survey of 164 Recovery Sex Addicts And Partners. *Sexual Addiction & Compulsivity*, 5: 189–217.

Steffens, B., & Means, M. (2009) *Your sexually addicted spouse*, New Horizon Press, Far Hills, NJ.

Part II
Socio cultural differences

Part II represents a significant addition to the original edition of this book. Over the years since the first edition was released, I have gained considerably more knowledge and experience of working with people from a variety of different social and cultural communities and have increasingly recognised the need for tailor-made services. We start this section with Chapter 6 where we explore the unique perspectives and therapeutic issues that arise when working with women with sex, porn and/or love addiction. In Chapter 7 we look at addiction through the lens of those who define themselves as gender, sexual or relationship diverse and the importance of maintaining an affirmative therapeutic stance. In this chapter we also consider the growing problems of Chem-Sex and how we can help those within that community and also provide help for people who define themselves as heterosexual and are confused by their same sex behaviours. Chapter 8 will provide information and tools for those within religious communities and the therapists who help them, and for clients who define themselves as spiritual or who are confused about the spiritual side of the 12-Steps. We end Part II with Chapter 9 where the growing problem of sex offending is explored and how this links with sex and porn addiction. It includes an outline of common offending behaviours and the essential additional principles professionals need to undertake when working with this client group.

6 Female sex and love addiction

In this chapter we will explore what has commonly become known as FSLA – Female Sex & Love Addiction. We will also look at the growing problem of pornography addiction amongst women and investigate the commonalities and differences between sex and porn addiction and love addiction. Whilst treatment protocols are similar, we will also highlight some key differences when working with women. This chapter will also be helpful when working with men who identify more closely to love addiction than sex addiction.

What is love addiction?

There has been little research on love addiction and consequently there is even more confusion as to whether or not this really is an 'addiction.' Whilst 'falling in love' may 'feel' like an addiction, as many romantics would testify, until recently there has been limited research to support that love can be addictive in the same way as chemical addictions. But one paper argues that there is now 'abundant behavioral, neurochemical and neuroimaging evidence to support the claim that love is (or at least that it can be) an addiction, in much the same way that chronic drug-seeking behavior can be termed an addiction,' (Earp et al., 2017). Whether you agree with this or not, for any client who seeks help, it's important that we understand their frame of reference and align our language to theirs and for many of those experiencing love addiction, it can feel quite different to the common presentations of porn and sex addiction.

The term love addiction is used to describe the obsessive and compulsive pursuit of a relationship, and some may frame it more as a romance, fantasy or intensity addiction. For some this will be serial monogamous relationships, for others it will be affairs outside of the primary couple relationship and for some it may be an unhealthy preoccupation with someone unobtainable, be that physically or emotionally. On the surface love addiction presents as a search for intimacy, but in reality it is the pursuit of the high of 'falling in love' that the love addict yearns for, rather than true connection with a partner, (Ferree, 2012).

Like many clients presenting with sex or porn addiction, love addiction has its roots in attachment impairments and early relational trauma, (Katehakis, 2017). As we explored in Chapter 3, when a child fails to receive the love, care and attention they need to grow and develop, they may turn to substances or behaviours for comfort, rather than people. Typically someone with love addiction will have experienced an enmeshed relationship with a parent. Enmeshment is a term used when a parent identifies too closely with a child and uses the child to service their own emotional needs, (Adams, 2011). Examples include overt or covert sexual abuse, relying on the child as a confidant, being overly competitive or treating a child as a surrogate partner. Whilst the growing child may interpret the relationship as loving and close, the lack of appropriate boundaries damages the child's ability to recognise and communicate their own needs and leaves them feeling violated and controlled. This can result in a futile attempt to recreate this parental relationship in adulthood, one where to be loved they must be good and always respond to the needs of others. The love addict develops a childlike dependence on the euphoria of receiving another's unrivalled attention and affection, even if that's only temporarily achieved. Subsequently the reality of a long-term relationship, where there is inevitable conflict and an expectation of equality, may be either avoided or sabotaged. Or the love addict finds themselves trapped in endless relationships where true intimacy can never be experienced due to the other's unavailability, such as someone who is already married, or abusive or another addict. Pia Mellody describes the two fears of someone with love addiction; firstly the conscious fear of abandonment and secondly an unconscious fear of intimacy. This hypothesis explains why so many love addicts develop relationships with someone who is love avoidant and may exhibit co-dependent characteristics, (Mellody, 2003).

Like sex and porn addiction, love addiction is characterised by a pattern of behaviour that feels out of control, behaviour that the addict is unable to stop in spite of significant harmful consequences. But it is the search for what is perceived as 'true love' and romance that they crave, rather than sex itself. Having said that, most people with love addiction will wrongly equate sex with love and hence will be highly sexual and they may also use sex or porn as a way of escaping the emotional pain of failing to find their perfect relationship. Like many sex addicts, part of the dopamine rush is also the thrill of the chase and the sense of power and affirmation they achieve when their prey is caught. But once caught, the sex addict will quickly move to someone else, whereas the love addict will want to maintain at least some kind of relational connection. In today's Internet age, maintaining that connection is easier than it ever has been and many with love addiction will be avid users of social media and online chat forums and dating sites to both catch and keep their romantic conquests.

Female porn addiction

Many people assume that pornography addiction is a uniquely male problem, especially as we're commonly told that men are more visually stimulated than women. Whilst there may be some truth in the stereotype, women are not blind and at many stages of their lives they have equal sexual desire and curiosity. It is known that more and more women are viewing porn, (Wright et al., 2013) though there is little published research on the number of women becoming addicted. However, online forums and self-help resources indicate that porn addiction amongst women is on the increase.

The rise in pornography use amongst women may be due to a number of factors. It could simply be that women are more comfortable talking about their pornography use than they were 20 years ago, or perhaps the growing industry of female-friendly porn, often created by women porn producers, has made porn more appealing. Whatever the reasons, the impact on the brain of heavy pornography use, as explored in Chapter 1, is as real for women as men, and the function of the addiction to regulate emotion is also equally relevant for both genders. However, when it comes to treatment, there are additional considerations to bear in mind when working with a female sex, porn or love addict.

Working with women

Historically, research suggested that sex and porn addiction was predominantly a male problem with only an estimated 8–20 percent of people seeking help being women. It has often been argued that the prevalence is probably higher, but women have more difficulty seeking help. Partly because of the lack of specialist services and also due to the additional stigma that women may face in admitting to 'out of control' sexual behaviours (Ferree, 2002). This is backed up by my UK survey where 25 percent of the survey respondents were women but 60 percent had never sought help, compared to 42 percent of men who had never sought help (Hall, 2013).

The stigma might also explain why more women present as love addicts than sex addicts, preferring to focus attention on the relational side of sex than the act of sex – 50 percent in my survey compared to just 13 percent of men (Hall, 2013). However, it's important not to make assumptions about the acting out behaviours of women, as much of it is similar to those of men. For example, watching pornography – 73 percent women, 89 percent men; fetish behaviours – 36 percent women, 24 percent men; stranger sex – 41 percent women, 32 percent men; and multiple affairs – 54 percent women, 37 percent men. In fact the only area where men differed considerably was in the use of sex workers with only 3.3 percent of women compared to 30 percent of men using their services (Hall, 2013).

When working with women with sex, porn or love addiction, there are three key areas that need additional consideration. We will look at each of these in turn:-

- *Socialisation* – Little girls are brought up with very different messages compared to little boys, especially around topics of sex and relationships. Historically women have been taught to be submissive to men and that their greatest goal in life should be to fall in love and live happily ever after. In our modern, equal opportunity society, it would be nice to think that much of this has changed, but regrettably most of us still live by a set of prescribed 'rules' for relationships that are gender specific and almost impossible to live up to (Barker, 2013). For many women struggling with addiction, their search for a perfect relationship that will rescue them from life's difficulties is one that has been imprinted from an early age and one that continues to be perpetuated on our screens and in the media. Whilst it's true that many men also struggle with the illusion that finding the 'right' partner will also make them whole, they are less likely to overtly use their sexuality to find that person.
- *Sexuality* – Like men, many women who struggle with sex, porn and love addiction struggle with low self-esteem and are desperate for approval. But unlike men, most women will have been brought up to believe their greatest asset and source of worth is their sexuality. Female sexuality is different from men's in many ways, not least of which is the fact that female sexual desire is impacted by menstruation. Many women are aware of their changing drive over the course of a month and many female porn addicts may notice that they are drawn to different genres of porn at different times.

- *Shame* – As we've said before, shame is the oxygen that fuels the fire of addiction and for women, the shame around sexual addiction is even greater. Our culture normalises men's proactive, or even aggressive, sex drive, but a women who openly expresses her sexual desire is more likely to be shamed and named a whore and an unsuitable life partner. Evidence suggests that sexual double standards have not subsided (Bordini and Sperb, 2013). For the female sex and love addict, desperate to meet Mr or Ms Right, their acting out behaviour perpetuates their shame as they increasingly believe they are unworthy of the love they seek. Furthermore, as our society becomes increasingly sexualised, a woman's worth is often calculated on the basis of her sexual attractiveness and women are encouraged to maintain their youth and beauty, whatever their age. This leaves many women with a conundrum – be sexy, but not a slut – and experiencing shame if they look too hot or too dowdy.

When working with women, socialisation, sexuality and shame all need to be viewed through a female lens, whilst also hearing the history and individual cultural experiences of the client. In addition to reducing shame, which we explore further in Chapter 10, clinicians also need to be aware of additional triggers linked to female sexualisation. For example, their own physical appearance may be a trigger, such as wearing clothes that make them feel more sexually confident or general grooming routines such as painting their nails, doing their hair or moisturising their skin can all be triggering activities. And a female client may need to maintain a menstruation diary to notice times of the month when she is more vulnerable to acting out. Whilst it's certainly not true for all, some love addicts may also be more vulnerable to seduction as this may have played a role in their acting out behaviours. Hence a clinician needs to be mindful of the possibility of being seduced and also of being perceived as a seducer.

Clinicians also need to consider different treatment regimes when working with women. It's been suggested that the female brain prefers to build relationships before following task-based recovery programmes and may find the immediate assigning of tasks dismissive and isolating (Katehakis, 2017). Therefore, therapists who are used to prescribing traditional CBT models may require more emphasis on individual, relational based therapies before moving on to behavioural recovery work.

References

Adams, K.M. (2011) *Silently Seduced: When parents make their children partners*, Health Communications Inc.

Barker, M.J. (2013) *Re-writing the Rules*, Routledge, London.
Bordini, G.S., & Sperb, T.M. (2013) Sexual Double Standards: A Review of Literature, *Sexuality & Culture*, 17(4): 686–704.
Earp, D., Wudarczyk, O., Foddy, B., & Savulescu, J. (2017) Addicted to love: What is love addiction and when should it be treated? *Philosophy Psychiatry and Psychology*, 24(1): 77–92.
Feree, M.C. (2002), Females – The forgotten Sex Addicts, in Carnes, P. & Adams, K.M. *Clinical Management of Sex Addiction*, Routledge, New York.
Feree, M.C. (ed.) (2012) *Making Advances: A comprehensive guide for treating female sex and love addicts*, Society for the Advancement of Sexual Health, Royston, GA.
Hall, P. (2013) *Understanding and Treating Sex Addiction*, Routledge, London.
Katehakis, A. (2017) *The female face of sex addiction: The Routledge International Handbook of Sexual Addiction*, Routledge, London.
Mellody, P. (2003) *Facing Love Addiction: giving yourself the power to change the way you love*, Harper One, New York.
Wright, P.J., Bae, S., & Funk, M. (2013) United States women and pornography through four decades: Exposure, attitudes, behaviors, individual differences, *Archives of Sexual Behaviour*, 42(7): 1131–1144.

7 Sexual diversities and ChemSex

In this chapter we will explore the unique needs of people who identify as gay, lesbian and bi as well as those who engage in kink and those in the ChemSex communities. The usual principles of assessment, as discussed in Part I, and the treatment strategies in Part III apply to sexually diverse clients, but additional issues relating to childhood and adolescent experience, self identity, relationships and sexual and lifestyle choices need to be considered.

Before launching into this chapter, I feel the need for a disclaimer. At the time of writing this book, our culture is experiencing a revolution of sexual identities, orientations and lifestyles. We have perhaps never had more sexual freedom than we have now, at this moment in history, to define ourselves as we wish and find others who think and feel like us. And as our sexual landscape grows, so does our language. The language we use to define ourselves is important, but varies hugely from community to community and around the globe. I have focussed this chapter on the language and terminology that is currently most familiar in my clinical experience – so whilst I speak of sexual diversity such as gay, lesbian and bi, that doesn't mean that transsexual, pansexual, asexual, mostly heterosexual, transgender, intersex, questioning and queer identities are any less important, but rather that they're not currently present in the clinical dialogues of sexual addiction. I have chosen to drop the language of paraphilia and fetish and instead refer to these as kink, though some professionals may prefer more traditional nomenclature. Like neuroscience, this is an area of life and therapy that is rapidly growing and changing, so please also hold in mind the time when this book was written.

Gay, Lesbian and Bisexual

As explored in the previous chapter, there has been little research with women who struggle with sex and porn addiction and there is even less for those who define themselves as lesbian or bisexual. Kasl suggests that there is often less stereotyping of an actively sexually addicted woman in the lesbian community (Kasl, 2002) and goes on to explain that there may be fewer internalised messages, compared to heterosexual women, of being a slut or a whore. She goes on to say that lesbian women may struggle with the notion of dependency within a relationship, be that relating to addiction or co-dependency, as they often shun heterosexual models of female dependency commonly found in heterosexual partnerships. Awareness of these differences in gender perception are important when understanding or working with any addictive or compulsive behaviour with lesbian or female bi clients.

Compared to heterosexuals, it's thought there is a greater incidence of sexual addiction among gay and bisexual men; one proposed explanation for this is that gay men have more sexual outlets and hence someone with a predisposition to compulsive behaviours is more likely to develop the condition if they're gay (Grov et al., 2010). On the whole, sex addiction does not change among different groups but the differences in cultural norms and developmental backgrounds must be recognised and understood in order to provide appropriate treatment within gay communities (Weiss, 2013).

Lesbian, gay and bisexual people have often come from a background of repressed gender orientation or identity issues, homophobic judgements, teasing, bullying and discrimination. Many also experience increased loneliness and low self esteem and difficult coming out stories, all of which can contribute to an increased likelihood of developing compulsive sexual behaviours (Chaney and Burs-Wortham, 2014). People within these communities may also have complex issues relating to sexual shame, much of which may have developed within the home and social environment whilst growing up, but may vary greatly depending on age, geographic location and social support networks. Notions of sexual sobriety tend to come from a hetero-normative, monogamous viewpoint and it's important to recognise that many sexually diverse clients may not agree with these. Every person needs to recognise their individuality and be free to define which of their behaviours they feel are damaging and compulsive and which are not.

Understanding MSM (Men who have Sex with Men)

MSM (Men who have Sex with Men) is a term that is generally used to describe heterosexual men who, recreationally, or compulsively have sex with other men. In some academic circles the term is used to describe all men who have sex with men, some of whom may identify as straight, gay or bi, but for the purpose of this chapter, I am referring to heterosexual men who have sex with men.

There appears to be no research on the number of straight men who have sex with men, though it is an area of increasing clinical research and representation. This is perhaps due to the reduced stigma of same sex relationships and sexual encounters and greater openness to sexual fluidity. In the field of sex and porn addiction, MSM is commonplace, whether that's a straight man watching gay porn or visiting saunas or meeting for casual sex on meet up apps such as Grindr. For some, this will be an escalation of behaviour as dopamine seeks greater and greater variety, while for others it may satisfy a sexual interest they've held for many years. For others, the behaviour may be linked to experiences of childhood sexual abuse. We talked about the links between childhood sexual abuse and sexual addiction in Chapter 3 and, as discussed before, acting out behaviours are often a way of unconsciously working through the trauma in an attempt to find resolution. Whilst abuse won't be present for all MSMs, it's crucial that this is explored and worked through as part of the recovery process.

For many of those who escalate to same sex behaviours, there are also practical reasons why they have sex with men. Finding same sex partners is easy and free, there are no expectations on either partner beyond the sexual exchange and for those in monogamous couple relationships it may feel less like betrayal as there is no comparison, nor competition, to the sexual relationship at home.

Whatever the reason for the behaviour, MSM can throw up questions of sexual identity for both the person with the addiction and the partner, leaving many worrying that the explanation for the behaviour is that they are gay, or at least bisexual.

In Joe Kort's excellent book, Is My Husband Gay, Straight or Bi (2014) he suggests the following areas of exploration to help those concerned about their, or their partner's, sexual orientation.

- *The beach test* – in an environment where both men and women are scantily clad, who do you notice first, the men or the women? Which gender do you feel instinctively attracted to?
- *Youthful noticing* – described as the children's version of the beach test, before the age of puberty, were you more drawn and intrigued by girls or boys? And were you more likely to obsess and become pre-occupied with male or female adults?
- *Waking up* – who do you want to wake up next to, a man or a woman? Who would you want to kiss first thing in the morning and cuddle up to?

- *Falling in love* – do you make romantic connections with men or with women? Over your lifetime, if you've thought about settling down into a committed relationship, has that been with a man or a woman?
- *Gay sex not degrading* – Kort describes how many MSMs feel shame about having sex with men and may feel degraded by it, whereas a gay man will be more likely to experience sex as natural and joyful.
- *Homophobia* – finally Kort reports that many gay men who are unconscious of their gayness and perhaps repressing it, tend to be more homophobic, whereas MSMs would generally feel content with being gay, but simply feel that they aren't.

Clearly these areas of exploration cannot provide a definitive answer for the client questioning sexual orientation and it must be remembered that orientation is a continuum that may change over our lifetime. Ultimately only the client can decide where they are on that continuum between straight and gay and exploration needs to take into consideration their individual social context and life experiences.

Whatever the explanation of MSM behaviour may be, if the behaviour is compulsive and unwanted and causing significant harmful consequences, then it can be worked with in the same way as other acting out behaviour.

Working with Kink

Kink is a term now commonly used to describe any sexual behaviour, fantasy or sexual lifestyle that is 'unconventional' – though conventions are constantly changing! The term embraces what others might define as a fetish, such as an attraction to latex, feet or body piercings, or a paraphilia such as BDSM, scatting or water sports. Kink also includes those who choose an alternative sexual lifestyle to societies' norms, such as polyamory, swinging or open non-monogamy. Some users of the kink definition prefer to use it exclusively to describe behaviours that, whilst unorthodox, enhance intimacy in sexual relationships rather than replace it.

Most kinks do not cause any emotional or psychological difficulty and indeed, many are now commonplace in society as we can see from high street stores such as Ann Summers and novels such as *Fifty Shades of Grey*. And for many, the choice to move away from terms such as paraphilia is a deliberate attempt to de-medicalise sexual behaviours that cause no harm. In an attempt to destigmatise non-normative behaviours,

DSMV 5 no longer lists paraphilias, but rather 'paraphilic disorders,' with the criteria that to be diagnosed as a disorder the behaviour must cause personal distress and/or be non-consensual, such as voyeurism, paedophilia and bestiality. The term 'sexual and erotic conflict' is often used to explain why some people struggle psychologically with their kink (Braun-Harvey et al., 2016). Sexual and erotic conflicts may be experienced within the self, and with others – whether that's within a partnered relationship or perceptions of societal acceptance. Working through these conflicts is an essential part of therapy with any client presenting with kink, especially those who believe their behaviour may be compulsive.

Some people with sex addiction experience no distress from their kink, whilst for others the kink behaviour is the main source of negative consequences. When this is the case, work can be done with a therapist to reduce dependency on the distressing stimulant and develop positive sexuality, as explored in Chapter 13, whereas those who experience no distress about their attraction will be happy to incorporate it into their recovered sexual lifestyle. On some occasions it is the partner who experiences the distress. During disclosure it may be revealed that the person with the addiction has a kink that they have privately and secretly engaged in outside of the relationship. Some partners may be able to accept a difference in taste but not want to participate, while others may be comfortable incorporating it into the relationship. If a behaviour can not be tolerated by a partner, for whatever reason, this should be respected and supported while considering what impact this may have on the viability of the relationship's future.

It is not understood how and why some people develop kinks and some do not. Our sexuality is highly complex and is influenced by many factors including hormones, childhood experiences, individual personality and relational and social contexts. There is some evidence that childhood trauma can result in development of a kink, but there are also many people with different sexual preferences with no history of abuse of any kind. Unfortunately, there are many who prefer to pathologise or ridicule people with different sexual tastes, rather than accept that human sexuality is still beyond our comprehension.

It is often a challenging task to decide if a kink is significant to the addiction or not and therapists should be competent at working in this field (Shahbaz and Chirinos, 2016). Many people feel shame about their 'unusual' attractions, a topic we refer to at length in Chapter 10, but that may be the result of societal, cultural and relational stigma rather than because the behaviour is compulsive. Therapy is often required to help to decide where the behaviour belongs in the two circle boundary exercise and, as always, ultimately the individual must decide if they want the behaviour to be part of their sexual repertoire as they move forward in their recovery.

ChemSex

It has been widely recognised for many years that drug use is higher amongst sexually diverse communities than in the heterosexual population (Sewell et al., 2017), but most recently, public health concerns have risen over a particular group of drugs and their link to the increased transmission of HIV, STIs and deaths caused by overdose. ChemSex is the term now widely used to describe a specific type of drug taking behaviour by gay men where three drugs are often taken simultaneously for the express purpose of enhancing sexual enjoyment and reducing inhibition (Bourne et al., 2014). These three drugs are often referred to as the Unholy Trinity and are:

- *Mephedrone* – often referred to simply as M, meow meow or M-Cat, a stimulant that makes you feel incredibly awake, euphoric and affectionate around people. Most often it is snorted, or sometimes injected. Within ChemSex communities, injecting is more often referred to as slamming. A common side effect is weight loss.
- *GHB/GBL* – known as G, a liquid that is taken in millimetre doses, usually put into another drink. It creates feelings of relaxation, self confidence and increases libido. It is highly addictive and even a ½ ml overdose can create a coma, often referred to as a G-sleep. It is particularly dangerous if taken with alcohol.
- *Crystal Meth* – most widely known as Tina, either smoked or injected. It creates euphoria and heightens arousal and libido. Side effects include agitation, paranoia and confusion.

Whilst the combination of these drugs increases sexual arousal and libido, the side effect of mephedrone and crystal meth is reduced sexual functioning, most commonly delayed ejaculation and erectile dysfunction, hence Viagra is also commonly used. Withdrawal can be severe after a weekend of ChemSex which means that many also use ketamine or valium to self-medicate the come down.

To give an indication of the growth of ChemSex culture, in 2005 these three drugs were responsible for 3 percent of all presentations among gay and bisexual men to the drug service Antidote, but by 2012 that figure had risen to 85 percent and use of these drugs is now almost exclusively within sexual settings (Stuart, 2013). However, ChemSex is about much more than the combination of drugs used, it's about the community that uses them, why they use them and how they're different from other drug users and sexual lifestyles.

ChemSex can occur in a variety of ways. Sometimes for lone masturbation, or most often, during partnered sexual encounters arranged on gay hook up apps such as Grindr, with either one or multiple partners over a 24–36 hour period. The 'wild' ChemSex party has received most media hype, sometimes referred to as 'chill outs' or 'PnP' (party and play), events that happen at people's homes and are promoted on social media, but in reality, these are more rare. For many gay and bisexual men, with a common history of being socially shunned and sexually rejected, ChemSex loosens inhibitions to facilitate hooking up with single or multiple partners for sexual marathons, where the sharing of drugs, as well as sex, builds intimacy and connection and offers sexual validation and affirmation. For men with low sexual self confidence and/or low body self esteem, it's a safe place for sexual expression and experimentation.

But as the drugs wear off, many will regret the weekend's events and experience confusion and shame and well as the physical come down. During this period, many delete or block any sexual partners they acted out with as a way of disconnecting and denying the events took place. During the high of ChemSex, there is a great sense of community and shared experience, but as reality dawns, there is a greater sense of isolation and feeling desperately alone.

People in the ChemSex community generally do not see themselves as having a drug problem, they perceive their drug use as purely recreational and an aid to facilitate their chosen sexual lifestyle. Whilst a growing number of people engaging in ChemSex approach sexual health services for support, this is rarely to give up their behaviour, but rather to receive treatment for sexual health concerns. However, a growing number are reporting negative consequences and a desire for change, but there are few services experienced in dealing with the unique biopsychosocial needs of this client group. In his book, Something for the Weekend, James Wharton suggests that the core motivators for becoming involved in ChemSex are; a desire to enjoy yourself; a tendency to self destruct, a means to escape the realities of life and self loathing, concluding that when these are combined with opportunity and a desire to connect, you get ChemSex.

Through extensive research, The Chemsex Study (Bourne et al., 2014) highlighted a number of areas of concern, many relating specifically to drug use, namely the fears of G overdose and managing increasing problems with come-downs, especially panic attacks and paranoia, while others focussed on sexual health and sexual functioning concerns, particularly losing the ability to enjoy sex without chems. Many interviewees lamented the impact on other areas of their life, such as not having time to spend on other activities or seeing friends and family. Perhaps most worryingly, many said they had either experienced, or witnessed, significant violations of sexual boundaries, which some framed as assault. When you combine the power of sexual disinhibition and raging libido, with lowered pain threshold and losing consciousness, a regular consequence is an inability to give consent, or recognise when someone is not able to give consent. This can cause considerable inter and intra psychic conflict when the drugs wear off and the community is left to consider if everyone at the party was truly a willing participant.

One of the key justifications of the ChemSex lifestyle is that it is an intrinsic part of being an urban gay man; to be able to enjoy sexual freedom without judgement or shame. But the growing number of sexual assault reports flies in the face of this thinking for many. What's more, two-thirds of the ChemSex Survey respondents said they were not happy with their sex life and what they desired was a long- term partner for more intimate and emotionally connected sex. Furthermore, while many used the ChemSex scene to bolster underlying psychological issues of low self esteem, many are beginning to recognise that ChemSex merely provides an escape, not a cure, and brings with it a whole host of additional problems.

Helping people trapped by ChemSex requires a multi-disciplinary approach. As well as educated sexual health support and competent drug awareness, clinicians also need to be psycho-sexually trained to help clients develop sober sexuality. As we will explore much further in Chapter 10, one of the biggest blocks to recovery for everyone with compulsive sexual behaviours is self-limiting beliefs. And for many in the ChemSex community, there is a belief that sex can no longer be enjoyable without drugs and that they will never be able to experience the joy of validation and intimate connection without them. A recovery community along with individual therapy is essential to break through these fears, alongside compassionate understanding of each individual's personal story and situation.

Therapeutic essentials within sexually diverse communities

Understanding a client's unique situation and circumstances, as well as their individual social context, is an important part of any therapeutic relationship, but when working with people who have historically been marginalised, abused and discriminated against, it is essential. Indeed failing to do so could not only fail to help the client reach their therapy goals, but do additional psychological harm.

Gender, sexual and relationship diversity, commonly referred to as GSRD (Davies and Barker, 2015) has now widely over taken the term gay-affirmative therapy to encompass a wider spectrum of sexual and gender identities and lifestyles. The principle of GSRD is that therapists need to develop a greater understanding of issues relating to clients with diverse identities as well as identifying and resolving their own personal bias. Below is a list of key issues for consideration. There is not space in this book to provide detailed information and guidance on each topic so therapists and health professionals may benefit from further reading and training and should check the latest information available from their professional body.

- *Internalised heterosexism* – sometimes referred to as internalised homophobia or internalised homonegativity, this term encompasses the many ways in which people from diverse communities are affected by negative family and societal messages about their identity. Clients need space to share their thoughts, feelings and experiences of what it means to be themselves. To explore how the views of family, peers and society at large, both today and throughout their childhood, have shaped their image of themselves. Negative messages, stigma and shame, all need to be addressed whilst supporting and affirming the client's identity.
- *Minority stress* – minority stress theory explains why some people from diverse sexual communities may develop sexually compulsive behaviours (Pachankis et al., 2015). The stress caused by being a minority group and facing a constant challenge and process of 'coming out' in a dominant hetero-normative society can result in long term emotional dysregulation. These stressors may be exaggerated for those within other minority groups such as race or ability. Therapists need to be aware of the multiple ongoing stressors as they relate to a client and help clients develop healthier emotional coping strategies tailored to their individual lifestyle and circumstances.
- *Hypervigilance* – because of the negative experiences so many diverse sexualities have had, many people develop a hypervigilance towards judgement and prejudice. This hypervigilance can cause feelings of stress and anxiety in almost all social situations or environments, including the therapy room. Therapists need to remain mindful of this and be sensitive in their language and ready to answer any questions that might arise.
- *Religion and spirituality* – organised religion has oppressed sexual diversity for centuries, and regrettably most still do. For clients with

a faith, this may feel particularly rejecting and isolating and create a further layer of guilt and shame. When working with addiction, therapists need to recognise the history of institutional oppression and collaborate with the client around appropriateness of seeking traditional 12-step support (Chaney and Burs-Wortham, 2017).

- *Sexual health* – as explored in the section on ChemSex, sexual health issues and concerns are commonplace, especially in clients whose behaviours have escalated into addiction. An awareness and comfort talking frankly about sexual practices and sexual health concerns can help to reduce stigma and shame as well as providing crucial psycho-education and guidance.

References

Bourne, A., Hammond, G., Hickson, F., Reid, D., Schmidt, A., & Weatherburn, P. (2013) *What constitutes the best sex life for gay and bisexual men? Implications for HIV prevention. BMC Public Health*, 13: 1083.

Bourne, A., Reid, D., Hickson, F., Torres Rueda, S., & Weatherburn, P. (2014) *The Chemsex study: drug use in sexual settings among gay & bisexual men in Lambeth, Southwark & Lewisham*: Sigma Research, London School of Hygiene & Trop Med. www.sigmaresearch.org.uk/chemsex

Braun-Harvey, D., & Vigorito, M.A. (2016) *Treating Out of Control Sexual Behaviour, Rethinking Sex Addiction*, Springer Publishing, New York.

Chaney, M.P., & Burs-Wortham, C.M. (2014) Examining coming out, loneliness and self esteem as predictors of sexual compulsivity in gay and bisexual men, *Sexual Addiction & Compulsivity*, 22(1): 71–88.

Chaney, M.P., & Burs-Wortham, C.M. (2017) Sexual compulsivity and men who have sex with men (MSM), in Birchard, T. & Benfield, J. (eds) *The Routledge International Handbook of Sexual Addiction*, Routledge, London: pages 305–316.

Davies, D., & Barker, M.J. (2015) Gender and sexuality diversity (GSD): Respecting difference, *The Psychotherapist*, 60: 16–17.

Grov, C., Parsons, J.T., & Bimbi, D.S. (2010) Sexual compulsivity and sexual risk in gay and bisexual men, *Archive of Sexual Behaviour*, 39(4): 940–949.

Kasl, C.S. (2002) Special issues in counseling lesbian women for sexual addiction, compulsivity, and sexual co-dependency, *Sexual Addiction & Compulsivity*, 9: 191–208.

Kort, J., & Morgan, A.P. (2014) *Is My Husband Gay, Straight or Bi? – A Guide for Women Concerned About Their Man*, Rowman and Littlefield, New York.

Pachankis, J.E., Rendina, H.J., Restar, A., Ventuneac, A., Grov, C., & Parsons, J.T. (2015) A minority stress emotion regulation model of sexual compulsivity among highly sexually active gay and bisexual men, *Health Psychology*, 34(8): 829–840.

Sewell, J., Miltza, A., Lampea, F.C., Cambianoa, V., Speakman, A., Phillips, A.N., Shahbaz, C., & Chirinos, P. (2016) *Becoming a kink aware therapist*, Taylor & Francis, London.

Stuart, D. (2013) Sexualised drug use by MSM: background, current status and response, *HIV Nursing*, Spring: 6–10.

Stuart, D., Gilson, R., Asboe, D., NwokoloN., Clarke, A., Collins, S., Hart, G., Elford, J., & Rodger, A. (2017) Poly drug use, chemsex drug use, and associations with sexual risk behaviour in HIV-negative men who have sex with men attending sexual health clinics, *International Journal of Drug Policy*, 43: 33–43.

Weiss, R. (2013) *Cruise Control, Understanding Sex Addiction in Gay Men*, Gentle Path Press, Arizona.

Wharton, J. (2017) *Something for the weekend, Life in the Chemsex Underworld*, Biteback Publishing, London.

8 Faith communities and spirituality

According to David Ley, the author of *The Myth of Sex Addiction*, sex and porn addiction are myths perpetuated largely by people and organisations with a religious agenda (Ley, 2014). There seems to be no evidence to support this claim, but it's certainly true that faith traditions are prominent in addiction recovery and advocacy, as they are in many other mental and social health arenas. Whatever the reality, or agenda, may be, the role of spirituality in addiction recovery is something that has been written about and worked with for many years, (Cook, 2004, Grodzicki, 2006). Furthermore, those of us who choose to help people in addiction recovery cannot avoid, nor would many want to, the influence of the 12-Step fellowships on developing and maintaining sobriety. Hence, an understanding of spirituality and its role in addiction recovery is essential. And for clients from faith communities it may be central to their personal identity, motivation and treatment requirements. In this chapter we will explore the role of spirituality in addiction and more specifically how to work with clients who present as people of faith.

Spirituality and addiction

Spiritual health is one of the four dimensions of well being as defined by the World Health Authority, the others being physical, mental and social. But defining spiritual health, or indeed, spirituality is not straightforward and controversy can arise when spirituality is confused with religion. For the purpose of this chapter, I would define spirituality as a distinctive, universal aspect of the human experience. It encompasses our subjective awareness of ourselves as unique individuals and our inner awareness of others and our relationships with them. It is the bit of ourselves, others and our world that we deem of critical importance and hence it is the part of us where we hold our inner sense of truth and from which we derive meaning and purpose for our lives. The Royal College of Psychiatrists' online booklet defines spirituality as:-

- a deep-seated sense of meaning and purpose in life
- a sense of belonging
- a sense of connection of 'the deeply personal with the universal'
- acceptance, integration and a sense of wholeness

And goes on to add that patients who say they have spirituality in their lives feel they have gained:-

- better self-control, self-esteem and confidence
- faster and easier recovery (often through healthy grieving of losses and through recognising their strengths)
- better relationships – with self, others and with God/creation/nature
- a new sense of meaning, hope and peace of mind. This has enabled them to accept and live with continuing problems or to make changes where possible

Over recent years there has been growing encouragement for mental health professionals to talk about spirituality with their clients and patients in an attempt to better meet their needs. One research paper found that whilst user surveys showed that up to half of patients turn to their religious and spiritual beliefs to help get them through a crisis, they did not feel comfortable talking about spirituality with their psychiatrist (Faulkner, 1997). Perhaps this should surprise us when we consider that the word 'psyche' comes from the Greek meaning, breath, life, soul – so those of us working as psychologists, psychiatrists or psychotherapists are deemed to be working with the spiritual dimension.

Religion and addiction

According to a YouGov survey in 2015, 32 percent of respondents believe in 'a god,' 20 percent believe in a 'higher power' of some sort and 14 percent are unsure. Only 32 percent believed there was no spiritual god or higher power (https://yougov.co.uk/news/2015/02/12/third-british-adults-dont-believe-higher-power/). If these statistics are to be believed then two thirds of our clients will believe, or wonder if, there is something outside of themselves, and other human beings, that has influence in their lives.

The key difference between religion and spirituality is that religion is organised. Organised into groups of people who share common beliefs, abide by common principles and engage in common spiritual practices as detailed in their communal rule book. Whilst there are some significant differences between religions and between various facets of each religion, what they all share is that they create a community. Some say that religion is itself a kind of addiction in so much as it creates the opportunity to escape from self (Birchard, 2017), but for many, like those who define themselves as spiritual, it provides a mechanism for developing a greater awareness of the self, others and the world within which they live.

The six largest religions in the UK are Christianity, Islam, Hinduism, Sikhism, Judaism and Buddhism, listed respectively in order of size. What they all have in common, with the exception of Buddhism, is that they all believe in one supreme, omnipresent God and that if you're not content with life, then you're not content with the God who gave you that life. They all believe in an afterlife, though for Buddhists and Hindus that sometimes means reincarnation back into this world until they reach Nirvana. All religions believe in good and evil and they all seek governance of the body over unhealthy appetites and list sex as one of those appetites. All faiths follow a similar tradition that if you put God first and live a virtuous life, then you will receive blessings, whether that's in this life or the next. And living a virtuous life means caring for self and others, doing good deeds and seeking to overcome negative character traits and behaviours; much of which is deemed to be possible by following religious practices such as prayer, meditation, fasting and fellowship with other believers, practices that have been shown to change brain function and improve mental and physical health (Cook et al., 2009).

For people of faith, addiction, of any kind, is a sin because it demonstrates an inability to manage life as God intended, that is, relying on Him for comfort not a chemical or behaviour. Furthermore, most religious doctrines place non-relational sex and lust as two of the greatest sins, though this will depend on interpretation of ancient scripts and is often linked to the views of religious teachers and leaders. For some people of faith, this means that masturbation is a sin, whilst for some, masturbation is only a sin if it's accompanied by lustful thoughts as opposed to focusing on physical release. For religious people who struggle with sex or porn addiction, and their partners, this can make this addiction a particularly shameful one and one less likely to be shared within the religious community.

Spirituality, religion, recovery and the 12-Steps

Part of me is uneasy about talking about the 12-Steps in this chapter, as it potentially continues the myth that they're only relevant to people of faith when in fact they can be an essential source of recovery for anyone and everyone. However, challenging the common misconceptions of the 12-Steps fits here, better here than anywhere else – and there's plenty more about their role in recovery in Part III.

The 12-Step programme was developed by Bill Wilson more than 75 years ago and while its strict tradition of ensuring anonymity makes it almost impossible to know how big the membership is, it's estimated to be over a million just in the US. Since its formation as AA, (Alcoholics Anonymous), it has gone on to provide self-help recovery communities for many other addictions, including gambling, narcotics, overeating, work, nicotine and sex and love addiction. Long-term efficacy is also difficult to measure, as it is in many areas of addiction treatment, but research suggests that the mechanisms used within 12-Step are effective at behaviour change (Best, 2017).

One of the biggest objections to the 12-Steps is the emphasis on relinquishing control to 'God' or a 'higher power,' though it's argued that at the root of this is not religion, but spirituality, which, for many, is expressed in the human connection found within a group (Kelly, 2017). For most people, even those with a rudimentary understanding of the 12-Steps, there is recognition that the fundamental principles make sense. Namely, recognising one's need for help and being willing to accept it, whether that means putting your faith in an omnipotent God, a spiritual 'higher power' or the community of the group you're a member of. One of the precepts of the 12-Steps is 'take what works, leave the rest.' While 12-Step groups continue to provide affordable, accessible, long-term support for people in recovery, this sounds like wise advice for anyone considering joining a group and for clinicians recommending them.

Working with people from faith communities

Many people with a faith choose to work with therapists from within their religious tradition or someone who views the world through a spiritual lens. Like others from minority communities, there is often the belief that they will receive less judgement and more understanding from a therapist who shares a similar perspective on life. But as we know, every human being is unique, whatever their sexuality, culture or creed and therefore, as clinicians, we must always confirm how clients identify themselves and what role spirituality or religion plays in their life. Whether or not you as a clinician define yourself as spiritual or religious, you may still find yourself working with clients who are. Some may ask about your personal views, others may not. Whether you choose to answer will depend largely on your therapeutic training as it would if you were questioned about your sexual orientation or whether you yourself are in recovery. Whatever your response, the following are areas for additional consideration when working with people of faith:-

- *The consequences of addiction* – As we've explored, for people of faith, addiction and sexual practices outside of their religious teaching are sins. This means that the experience of shame may be even greater for a religious person. Not only will they be grappling with their own sense of judgement and that of their family and loved ones, but also the judgement of their God and religious community. And when it comes to harmful consequences, some religions will believe the consequences of continuing addiction could affect them in the next life, not just the current one, and may have a direct impact on their descendants.
- *Hypocrisy* – Feeling a hypocrite is something experienced by many people struggling with addiction, and the partners who choose to stay in the relationship, but for people within religious communities, especially those in leadership, it may be worse. Many religions assign greater accountability to those in spiritual leadership roles, which means that someone with an addiction may feel they have to relinquish their position within their community because of their addiction. For some, for example Christian clergy, that may mean resigning from their parish and losing their home as well as their career. Honesty and integrity are highly treasured values within most religions and hence many addicts will need to make difficult decisions about who to share their addiction and recovery journey with, in order to remain within their fellowship with integrity.
- *Cognitive distortions* – Most faiths have similar traditions around repentance of sins, namely demonstrating remorse, praying for forgiveness and restoring healthy spiritual practices. When this has been achieved, once again the believer can receive the love and blessings of their God. Regrettably, for some, this can be used as a convenient loophole for continuing to relapse, as they know they can always repent and come back to God. In these situations, additional focus on other harmful consequences and life goals can help clients to develop stable recovery.

- *Positive sexuality* – There's much more on this in Chapter 13, but as when working with people from sexually diverse communities, the definition of 'positive' sexuality may be different for someone of faith. Some therapists may feel that the religious definition is restrictively narrow and struggle to help clients reach their personal objectives. Further reading on celibacy can be helpful to both the client and the therapist.
- *Spiritual recovery tools* – Whilst the religious addict may present with greater shame, a potential eternity of harmful consequences and restricted access to sexuality, they also come with an additional tool kit of recovery resources. Any spiritual practice can be used in relapse prevention, whether that's to reduce urges or divert to other dopamine inducing activities such as meditation or worship. And fundamentally, true faith in an almighty God who offers the strength you lack, and perhaps works miracles, can be trusted to beat any addiction.

References

Best, D. (2017) Why the mechanisms of 12-Step behaviour change should matter to clinicians, *Addiction*, 112: 938–939 . *doi: 10.1111/add.13631*.

Birchard, T.B. (2017) *The Routledge International Handbook of Sexual Addiction*, Routledge, London.

Cook, C.H. (2004) Addiction and Spirituality, *Addiction*, 99(5): 539–551.

Cook, C., Powell, A., & Sims, A. (eds) (2009) *Spirituality and Psychiatry*. RCPsych Publications.

Faulkner, A. (1997) *Knowing Our Own Minds*, Mental Health Foundation.

Grodzicki, J., & Galanter, M. (2006) Spirituality and Addiction, *Substance Abuse*, 26(2).

Kelly, J. (2017) Is Alcoholics Anonymous religious, spiritual, neither? Findings from 25 years of mechanisms of behaviour change research, *Addiction*, 112: 929–936.

Ley, D. (2014) *The Myth of Sex Addiction,* Rowman & Littlefield, Maryland.

Royal College of Psychiatristshttp://www.rcpsych.ac.uk/mentalhealthinfo/treatments/spirituality.aspx

9 Sex offending

All clinicians working in the field of sex and porn addiction need to be aware, and ready to work with, or refer, individuals with sex-offending behaviours and establish appropriate confidentiality contracts and supervision. Some clients will confess offending behaviours in the initial enquiry, or during the first session. But others may spend many weeks or months gaining the trust of the therapist before hinting at the extent of their acting out. In this chapter we will outline the key areas for consideration when working with people who offend and provide further resources for reading and guidance for those who choose to work with offenders.

What is sex offending

The term 'sex offender' might be used for anyone who has committed any kind of sexual offence and for most people, the term stirs a range of uncomfortable emotions including fear, disgust and anger. It's difficult to talk about sex offending without incurring moral judgement as most sexual offences involve a degree of coercion, or lack of consent. Consequently, sex offenders are a common target for societal moral outrage and are often forced to live with high levels of stigma and shame, whatever their crime may have been. But in reality, there is a wide range of sexual offending behaviours, some of which are deemed simply misguided and naïve horseplay and others that are morally reprehensible.

Sex offending includes both contact offences, such as rape and child sexual abuse, and non-contact offences such as voyeurism, exhibitionism and illegal pornography. The majority of people who present for sex and porn addiction therapy and are offenders report non-contact behaviour, and my practice does not work with contact offenders. Therefore what follows is an outline of non-contact, primarily internet, sex offences. Readers should be aware that the law varies around the world, and is regularly updated – what follows here is from a British perspective at the time of writing this book.

The most common type of offending behaviour occurs online when viewing illegal images. Illegal online images broadly fall into two categories, those deemed to be 'extreme pornography' and those that depict sexual images of children and adolescents under the age of 18, now often referred to as CSA images. Extreme pornography is listed within the Criminal Justice and Immigration Act 2008 and includes the viewing of images that are intended to create sexual arousal that show realistic scenes of serious injury to the genitals, anus or breasts, threat to life and rape. The law is complex to uphold as it must be proved that the images are showing non-consensual sexual acts and this has understandably led to concern from some kink communities who fear their chosen, consensual behaviours, such as BDSM (Bondage, Domination, Submission, Masochism) are being criminalised. Extreme pornography also includes sexual acts where consent is not possible, such as with an animal or a corpse. The viewing of CSA images is governed by the Protection of Children Act (1978/2012) and the Criminal Justice Act (1988/2002) and includes any indecent image, including photographs, pseudo-photographs and cartoons, whether moving or still, of someone under the age of 18.

Again, the law is complicated as the definition of 'indecent' is for the court to decide and hence there has been a backlash from some within naturist and artistic communities who fear they could be at risk of prosecution. For all categories of illegal pornography, the law criminalises making, distributing, downloading and viewing these images. As stated in Chapter 1, in the survey of 350 self-reporting sex and porn addicts, 43 percent had viewed either child or animal pornography (Hall, 2013), and in my clinical experience since writing this book, I would add that 1 in 10 of those would have viewed an underage image.

In addition to illegal pornography, another area that is common within sex addiction clients is exhibitionism and voyeurism. The Internet and smart phone technology has facilitated a growth in these behaviours in ways that were hitherto impossible. For example, a common form of voyeurism is what's known as 'up skirting.' This involves running the video function on your camera phone whilst attached to a selfie stick and carrying it at ground level directed up the skirts of unsuspecting people. Or the video function can be used whilst the phone is positioned under a changing room or toilet door. The camera phone can also be used for exhibitionism, often referred to now as cyber-flashing. This is when someone sends an unwanted sexual image of themselves to someone, sometimes using local networking facilities such as Air Drop. The Internet can also be used for exhibitionism through the use of webcams and posting on social media sites. In my survey 18 percent had engaged in exhibitionist or voyeuristic behaviours (Hall, 2013), but I suspect that figure would be much higher now that technology has improved. From my clinical experience I also know that many who engage in these activities are completely unaware that they are committing a sexual offence and could end up on the sex offender register. Furthermore, clients who look at pornography and masturbate in public places, such as in their car or garden or Public Park, assuming they cannot be seen, will rarely consider they could be prosecuted for exhibitionism if they were.

Whilst all of the scenarios above are classified as sexual offending, they do not all carry the same sentencing penalties. For example, someone caught cyber-flashing may just receive a verbal warning if it's deemed a one-off and non-aggressive event. Whereas someone reported for masturbating in their car within the vicinity of a primary school could receive a custodial sentence. Prosecution also varies with the viewing of CSA images – for example, whilst, technically, a 17 year old who takes a picture of their genitals and shares with their peers would have produced and distributed child pornography, they would probably receive a warning and advice on how to protect themselves, as well as others. Whereas someone who is found in possession of thousands of images of pre-pubescent children being forced into sexual acts would most likely receive the strongest sentence possible. Clinicians need to be aware of this wide range of offending behaviours and their legal and sentencing implications when considering which clients they can ethically work with.

Why people offend

At the time of writing this book, the media is awash with accusations of sexual abuse and celebs checking themselves into sex addiction rehabs in the States. Questions about the similarities and differences between sex offending and sex addiction are common on TV and radio chat shows and understandably there is a public backlash against the addiction label being used as an excuse for predatory, offending behaviour. There is an overlap between sex addiction and sex offending, in terms of both predisposing factors and genetic components (Smith, 2017a). However, there is a significant difference between those who offend as a consequence of the escalation process of non-offending sex or porn addiction and those who offend due to their primary sexual arousal template, incorporating a significant sexual attraction to children and/or young people, or because they enjoy the power that their predatory behaviours provide. Whilst the end behaviour may be the same, the motivation is very different. For example, a paedophile who is convicted of viewing underage images has a primary arousal template toward pre-pubescent children. They are not attracted to adults, but to children and hence their motivation comes from sexual arousal. There are of course paedophiles who never act out on their impulses because they are aware that to act out these impulses would be morally wrong and harmful to children. For those addicted to porn, the escalation process of the addiction, as explored in Chapter 1, together with the clever use of file-sharing, advertising pop-ups and reassuring viewing statistics, may lure them to viewing illegal images. The motivation is dopamine's search for novelty, not sexual attraction. But whatever the motivation, if a law has been broken then full responsibility needs to be taken and the consequences accepted. In the same way as someone found guilty of drink driving must pay the price, regardless of whether they are an alcoholic, irresponsible or indifferent to the law.

Before discussing confidentiality and contracting, it's important for clinicians to be clear about the client group they are choosing to work with, as this will direct the type of therapy and further training that may be required. I hope the following three statements will help to clarify?

- *I work with people with sex and porn addiction who have escalated to non-contact offending behaviours.* If this describes you, then there is plenty of additional help and resources in this book. The focus of work will be on addressing the addiction whilst maintaining an awareness of possible denial, cognitive distortions and risk, in specific relation to sexual offending.
- *I work with contact and non-contact sex offenders who want to stop, but have become addicted to their behaviours?* If this describes you then you'll find the recovery resources on addiction helpful, but also consider additional specialist sex offender training with organisations such as StopSo, and reading *Counselling Male Sexual Offenders: A Strengths-Focused Approach* (2017b) by Andrew Smith.
- *I work with repeat sex offenders, both contact and non-contact, who demonstrate limited remorse or motivation to stop.* This work is primarily undertaken by probation and the criminal justice system. You can also find more information and resources in the above text book by Andrew Smith.

Confidentiality

Many therapists and organisations are confused about their legal and ethical duty to report offending behaviours that are disclosed during therapy. At the current moment in time, therapists within the UK do not have a 'legal' responsibility to disclose online sex offending behaviours. However, we do have an 'ethical' responsibility to disclose if, by doing so, we can prevent immediate risk of harm to the client or to another. The difficulty with internet offences, including the viewing of CSA images, is that the harm has already occurred and reporting the viewer of the crime scene cannot prevent that harm. Most therapists only consider breaching confidentiality when children are, or may, be involved in the activity. For many therapists, not disclosing viewing CSA images is a difficult issue to square up morally as it can feel that not reporting is condoning the sexual exploitation of children. Some believe that if we can catch the people who view illegal images then we can stem the production of them. When making a decision whether to disclose to the authorities, therapists must consider their professional bodies code of ethics and be aware that if they do breach their client's confidentiality, they will need to demonstrate that they did so because they believed they could prevent imminent harm. Breaching client confidentiality because you feel 'it's the right thing to do' is not a sufficient retort and hence could result in a complaint against you being upheld.

The exception to this is where the confidentiality contract explicitly states the terms under which confidentiality will be breached. Many organisations hold policies stating that they will disclose to the appropriate authorities any client who has viewed child pornography, though few state what age of child this refers to. Furthermore, few make reference to viewing other illegal images or engaging in other non-contact offences such as voyeurism and exhibitionism, which, as we have seen, is commonplace.

The ethical dilemma for clinicians is further confused when one considers what impact their confidentiality policy may have on the client and on their ability to receive help and stop offending. Many believe it is better to maintain confidentiality in order to help clients to stop offending, rather than deter clients from reaching out for help; or forcing them to maintain a shameful secret throughout the therapeutic process which may impair their recovery from non-offending as well as offending behaviours. It should be remembered that some clients will only reach out for help once they have crossed the line into offending. For many, this is their rock bottom moment and a pivotal opportunity to break their addiction and achieve full recovery, which will not only benefit them, but also those who love and care for them.

A common misconception is that people who view CSA images will go on to abuse a child, though there is little evidence to support this. But even if this were the case, it could be argued that early confidential intervention is essential. Most research suggests that internet offenders who have no previous history of violence or antisocial behaviour and no convictions for offending, are at low risk of committing a contact offence with a child (Seto and Eke, 2005, Webb et al., 2007). However, low risk is not the same as no risk, and therefore therapists who choose to work with people who have viewed CSA images need to be aware of relevant risk factors.

Risk assessment with people who have viewed CSA images

Risk assessment is not a one-off event, but rather a process that needs to be undertaken throughout therapy. Furthermore, risk assessment should include someone other than a therapist. Regrettably, deceit and denial are common in all forms of addiction and hence therapists must not assume they are hearing the full story. What's more, one of the core personal requirements for being a therapist is having a natural tendency towards unconditional positive regard and empathy, which means we may not want to hear that our client is doing something wrong. Supervision is vital for any therapist, but when working with offenders it is even more critical. And if possible, someone outside of the organisation who is proficient within the field of offending should also be sought for consultation.

It's also essential to be aware that on-going risk assessment will be required when working with those who are already within the criminal justice system, as well as those who are not. When a client presents whom the authorities already know, this can create a false level of comfort for the therapist who may assume the police, probation or social services hold the responsibility for risk. But as a therapist, you may hear additional information that the authorities are not aware of which you may have a responsibility to report; for example, if probation conditions or child protection plans are being breached.

It is not the aim of this chapter to provide a thorough risk assessment protocol, and indeed it could be dangerous to do so, as external verification should always be sought as explained above. However, the following are areas of exploration that can be helpful and also guide a clinician towards making the decision on how to work with a client or whether to refer.

1. How old are the minors in the images that have been viewed?
2. What was the nature of those images, for example were they still naked images or moving images of a child being forced into a sexual act?
3. How long has the client been viewing these images and how regularly?
4. Has the client ever shared CSA images?
5. Does the client have any history of violent, anti-social or offending behaviour?
6. Has the client ever tried, online or offline, to initiate a sexual relationship with a minor?
7. Does the client have any significant psychological problems?
8. Does the client have any concurrent addiction problems that might further disinhibit behaviour, such as alcohol addiction?
9. Does the client have contact with any children of a similar age to those they were viewing?
10. How does the client feel about the images they have seen?
11. Does the client demonstrate motivation for change, beyond not getting caught or reducing a possible sentence?
12. What external authorities are involved and is the client willing to let you liaise with those authorities?

This list of questions is not meant to be exhaustive and all therapists and organisations should consult before developing a risk assessment strategy – and remember that risk assessment is on-going as further information may be revealed and client circumstances can change.

Therapeutic essentials when working with offenders

All effective therapy is based on establishing a firm therapeutic alliance. If a therapist feels unable to do this, due to their own feelings about a client's offending behaviours, or because of the client's emotional availability for therapy, then the case is probably best referred. As we explore in much greater depth in Chapter 10, reducing shame is critical to recovery from sex and porn addiction and never more so than in working with those who have offended. As with all clients, developing an understanding of what has caused and maintained the behaviour is essential to their recovery, as is exploration of why the offending happened, and why that particular type of offending, and, of course, developing strategies to stop all acting out, and prevent further acting out from occurring.

When a client presents who is already within the criminal justice system, there can be significant additional anxiety about the impact of prosecution. For most people, being sentenced for a sexual offence will probably mean losing their job and almost certainly their social status and reputation. It is common for the local press to name and shame and hence it may be impossible for the client to maintain any privacy. It can take between three months and two years for the forensic investigations to be completed and a final decision to be made. This is a hellishly long time for a client to not know what their future may hold. And of course, these doubts and fears extend to partners and family members as well. If the client has children then social services will almost certainly be involved and contact with children may be limited to supervised access only until the final court hearing. Regrettably there are many stories of people who have chosen to take their own lives rather than face, or live with, the consequences of their behaviour, therefore the potential risk of suicide needs to be taken very seriously with this client group.

Working with those who offend can be particularly challenging for therapists. Whilst emotional support can be provided and help given to develop greater personal understanding and insight, it can be difficult to hold on to hope, for both client and therapist. Working with remorse, regret and shame is always challenging, but when it can be balanced with a positive future focus on living a recovered life, then the outcome makes the challenge worthwhile. Regrettably the future is often very challenging for someone who serves time in prison for committing a sexual offence or for someone whose name will appear on the sex offender register. And until that decision is made by the court, all a therapist can do is help the client live with the unknown.

Finally, as stated earlier, risk assessment needs to be ongoing and for those working with clients who are already within the criminal justice system, consideration will need to be given to whether or not you will be willing to submit a court report. If you choose not to write a report, remember that your therapy notes can be subpoenaed so meticulous records should be kept.

References

Hall, P. (2013) *Understanding and Treating Sex Addiction*, Routledge, London.

Seto, M.C., & Eke, A.W. (2005) The criminal histories and later offending of child pornography offenders, *Sexual Abuse: A Journal of Research and Treatment*, 17: 201–210.

Smith, A. (2017a) Sexual Addiction & Sex Offending, in Birchard, T. & Benfield, J. (eds) *The Routledge International Handbook of Sexual Addiction*, Routledge, London: pages 362–372.

Smith, A. (2017b) *Counselling Male Sexual Offenders: A Strength-Focused Approach*, Routledge, London.

StopSo, Specialist Treatment Organisation for the Prevention of Sex Offending, contact info@stopso.org.uk.

Webb, L., Craissati, J., & Keen, S. (2007) Characteristics of internet child pornography offenders: a comparison with child molesters, *Sexual Abuse: A Journal of Research and Treatment*, 19: 449–465.

Part III
The C.H.O.I.C.E. recovery model

This is the part of the book that is full of the practical strategies and techniques for recovery from sex and porn addiction. It has been written primarily for people in recovery and for therapists who want down-to-earth advice on how to help. The acrostic CHOICE represents both the spirit and the stages of recovery. You can 'choose' a better life, it may be hard work, there may be twists and turns on the journey, but ultimately it's a choice. Our first chapter, Chapter 10, begins by explaining how to overcome the common faulty core beliefs that so often block the recovery journey and Chapter 11 focuses on building a vision for the future to build motivation and provide direction. In Chapter 12 you'll find the nuts and bolts of relapse prevention, along with further neurological and psychological explanations of why triggers and craving can sometimes feel so overwhelming. Identifying positive sexuality is the topic for Chapter 13 where you'll find information and guidance on how to find, and enjoy, sexual behaviours that fit with your value system and goals for the future. Relationships of all types are explored in Chapter 14, along with an explanation of why these are so important for mental health and we also look at the many benefits of being part of a recovery community. We end with Chapter 15, Establish confident recovery, where we look at how to manage any possible slips or relapses on the journey, as well as the essential lifestyle changes that can stop them from happening in the first place.

10 The C.H.O.I.C.E. recovery model
Challenge core beliefs

There are only two reasons why human beings ever change. Either the pain of staying the same is so great that they have to change, or they have a vision of something better. Change is a 'choice,' but before you can make that choice you have to root out any faulty core beliefs and thinking patterns that might be blocking your ability to recognise it as a choice, beliefs that might be telling you that you can't have a better life than the one your addiction has given you. There are many different core beliefs that block recovery. Some are spoken out-loud, others either whisper or scream silently in our heads. Broadly speaking, all of the beliefs that block recovery fall under three headings; 'I don't need to change,' 'I don't want to change' and 'I can't change.' We will look at each of these in turn now:-

I don't need to change

When someone with an addiction says 'I don't need to change' we call it denial and denial is by far the biggest cognitive block to recovery. Denial is often confused with deceit, but whereas deceit means lying to others, denial is when we lie to ourselves. Denial incorporates many different emotions and cognitions, some obvious, some subtle, but all either deny the consequences of the addiction altogether, or deny the impact of the consequences.

The importance of acknowledging and breaking denial is the essential first step of the 12-Steps. Step 1 says 'we admitted we were powerless over addictive sexual behaviour – that our lives had become unmanageable.' This step is often confused and conflated with a refusal to accept responsibility for acting out behaviours, but that is not what is meant. Admitting powerlessness means acknowledging that you cannot beat this addiction with self-control alone and recognising that craving is a force greater than your best intentions. Admitting that life has become unmanageable means accepting that if you want to feel in control of your life again, then you do have to change. Step 1 challenges us to accept powerlessness over our addiction, not powerlessness over our life. So why is denial so hard to break? And why do people ignore or minimise the negative consequences of their behaviour?

On the whole, us humans are a pretty resilient species but unfortunately that can go against us when it comes to beating addiction. Most of us have at least some success at leaving painful memories in the past and healthy optimism allows us to forge ahead with life without constantly worrying about what's round the corner. In some respects, people with a healthy resilience to life, who also struggle with addiction, can be the hardest to treat. It may be that a crisis of some sort is what initiated seeking help but when life is back on track, the pain may be forgotten and the initial incentive to change lost. Simply put, stressing about the potential consequences may not be in that person's nature.

Another common accompaniment to this kind of denial is the cognitive distortion of minimisation. Acting out behaviours may have been reduced so they're 'not that bad' and hence risk may be seen to be minimised as well. Some people with this denial are in the honeymoon period of recovery and having survived what they thought might be the end of their life as they knew it, feel temporarily safe. In short, they 'got away with it' and may feel that as long as they're careful, they can continue to 'get away with it.' Ultimately, it is, of course, the individual's prerogative to choose if they want to recover completely from their addiction or just cut down, but before making that decision, it's important to have all the facts and to have considered every possible outcome. To do this, both the actual and the potential consequences of continuing the addictive behaviour need to be considered.

Box 10.1 is an exercise that provides an opportunity to list the worst consequences of past acting out behaviour and to remember the feelings associated with the event then, and also now.

There is something incredibly powerful about seeing the worst pain of the past all written down in black and white along with its emotional impact. What most people find as they consider how they feel now when they reflect is that much of the pain is the same. A few express relief that the secrecy is over and the truth has been revealed, but the pain often does not diminish. In some senses, completing this exercise is a bit like returning to the scene of the crime or going back to the wreckage of the car. You may have survived, but the devastation is no less real. When completing this exercise with someone who has either a trauma or attachment-induced addiction, be prepared for the return of powerful negative emotions. Feelings of anxiety and/or attachment pain may resurface and will need to be soothed in a healthy way to avoid slipping back into denial.

> **Box 10.1 Rock bottoms**
>
> Take a sheet of paper and write down four or five of the rock bottom times that have been caused by your sex or porn addiction. They may be rock bottom because of an actual physical consequence, such as losing your job or going into debt, or because of the pain caused to a loved one, or of course both. Or it might be a rock bottom moment that was purely emotional – such as the terror you felt when you nearly got caught or the acute sense of shame you felt around a particular event, such as missing a special occasion because of your addiction or having to pretend to be someone you're not. In your mind's eye, go back to each of those times and write down every precise detail of what happened. As well as writing the facts, also write down exactly how you felt while it was happening and how you felt over the subsequent hours and days. When you have completed this, spend some time reading back over the rock bottom events you've listed and write down how you feel now as you bring them back into your conscious memory. Once you've done that, take another sheet of paper and write down how each of those events could have been worse. How much worse might you have felt if x, y or z had happened? If it's not possible for those events to have been any worse, ask yourself how many times you are willing to put yourself through those emotions? And how many times you're willing to put loved ones through those emotions?

Once the past consequences have been assessed, the potential cost of continuing to act out needs to be explored. Potential consequences in the future are perhaps more important to consider than past ones that can no longer be changed. What's more, we all make choices based on 'what-ifs,' for example just because someone has not yet been killed roller skating in the fast lane of the motorway does not mean it's a safe sport. For many people with sex or porn addiction, the potential consequences would increase considerably if their behaviour was known, for example if a partner, child or boss at work found out. The following exercise can be useful to provide the information required to ensure the risks of continuing to act out are fully calculated.

Box 10.2 Harmful consequences

On a scale of 1 to 10, where 1 is no risk at all and 10 is inevitable, complete these tables.

What is the risk of the following happening if you are found out   1 2 3 4 5 6 7 8 9 10

Hurting people you love

Not developing a relationship

Spending less time with people you love such as a partner, family and friends

Spending less time on health, hobbies and personal growth

Wasting money

Compromising your work, career or study

Catching, or transmitting an STI

Developing a sexual dysfunction

Being assaulted or assaulting someone else

Escalating alcohol or drug use

Damaging your self esteem

Hurting people you love

Losing your partner

Having less contact with your children or other family members

Losing friends

Losing your home

Losing your job

Reducing your disposable income

Being prosecuted

Damaging your self esteem

Wanting to end your life

Completing these exercises can serve as a harsh reality check, especially if completed with a trusted friend, therapist or 12-Step sponsor who can challenge any minimisations or other cognitive distortions. Although there may be a sense of 'getting away with it now,' is that really true? Is there really no cost or is it being denied? And what would the cost be of getting caught? Is it worth the risk? If the answer is yes, then perhaps the next core belief needs to be explored.

I don't want to change

If the consequences, actual and potential, have been accurately calculated, but there's still ambivalence about change, then recovery may not seem worth it. Beneath this thinking there is often a terrifying fear of loss. It's important to acknowledge that part of recovery includes loss and it is often this loss that feels 'not worth it.' That may be loss of sexual excitement, loss of freedom, loss of power or loss of self-identity. These feelings of loss need to be taken seriously, empathised with and mourned – and where possible, rebuilt or replaced. This can be particularly difficult when the benefits of recovery are a lifestyle that has never been experienced, not even as part of a double life. This is particularly true for people with porn addiction who have remained single and never had flesh on flesh sex with a human being.

> **Geoff's story**
>
> Geoff had always been a successful ladies' man. He had been a very attractive boy who grew into a very good-looking man and he had never been short of female attention. He loved women and he loved sex – and he had enjoyed plenty of both. He recognised he was addicted in his early 30s as his increasing efforts to commit to a steady relationship failed. Geoff had a few attachment issues as the result of seeing his parents' marriage fail, but primarily his addiction was opportunity-induced. He had the looks, the charm, the money and a job that gave him ample access to what he called 'an endless flow of willing pussy.' A year into recovery, Geoff had 'cut back' considerably, but he was still acting out. As much as he longed for a committed relationship and children, he couldn't imagine only ever sleeping with one woman. He also worried that without the drive to conquer and the thrill of the chase, he would become boring. He wondered if he was just one of those people who were born to be a Lothario and perhaps he should focus his therapy on mourning the fact that he might never have a 'normal' life.

Geoff's story illustrates another common faulty core belief that can keep people trapped in sex addiction and that is when they believe that sex is their greatest need. This is often a deeply held view for people who've been unable to experience intimacy or validation through any other kind of human connection and also for those who continue to believe that they have an exceptionally high sex drive. Psycho-education and CBT, (Cognitive Behavioural Therapy), can be helpful in recognising the difference between libido and craving and also understanding how the meaning they attribute to sex has influenced their feelings. There's more on this in Chapter 13.

Motivational Interviewing skills can be particularly beneficial for clients who are ambivalent about change. When a client can be helped to see the contradictions between their desires in a non-confrontational way they are more likely to open up to the idea of change and the next chapter 'Have a Vision' provides tools to help explore the benefits of overcoming addiction. But sometimes saying 'I don't want to change' is a defence mechanism against facing our deepest fears – those that tell us we 'can't change.' If we don't address these, changing our life and choosing recovery feels like nothing more than an empty dream rather than an achievable reality.

I can't change

If you lightly scratch the surface of any 'I can't change' statement you'll find a plethora of faulty core beliefs, and if you dare to dig deeper you may well find a cavern of shame. According to the great guru Patrick Carnes, sex addiction starts with faulty core beliefs (Carnes, 2001), and unless these beliefs can be re-written, the wheels of the addiction cycle will continue to turn. And if those faulty core beliefs are written so deeply that they've become scars, then you'll experience shame, which will continue to whisper 'you can't do it' or even 'you're not worth it.'

Our core belief system forms the cornerstones of how we think about ourselves, how we think about others and how we view our world. Our thoughts, feelings and behaviours are all defined by our belief system, even though some of those beliefs may be outside of our conscious awareness. Faulty core beliefs lie at the root of maladaptive thought patterns and, as any CBT therapist will know, it is those thoughts that influence how we feel and subsequently how we behave. In essence it is how we think about a situation that most deeply affects us, not the situation itself. And those negative thinking patterns directly influence how we behave. For example, if I think I am useless in social situations

I may feel anxious and self-conscious, then when I go to a social event I'm likely to behave in a shy and awkward manner and hence reinforce my belief that I'm useless in social situations. Our faulty core beliefs have an irritating ability to become self-fulfilling prophecies. Hence failing to challenge 'I can't change' is likely to lead to repeated slips and relapses.

Most of our core beliefs are formed in early childhood and someone with an attachment or trauma-induced addiction will most likely have developed faulty core beliefs that need to be identified and changed. For example, someone with an attachment-induced addiction who was neglected and not praised as child may grow up believing they're not worthy of love. And someone with a trauma-induced addiction who was the victim of bullying or abuse may grow up feeling alienated from others and unable to protect themselves. These faulty core beliefs are then reinforced by the addictive behaviour as the multiple affairs of attachment-induced addiction leave someone feeling increasingly unworthy of the love of their partner and people with a trauma-induced addiction feel isolated and ashamed of their addiction to dominatrix sex.

The picture is slightly different for someone with an addiction that was primarily induced by opportunity, who may have grown up with a relatively healthy set of core beliefs. But as they spiral into addictive behaviours their view of themselves may change as they no longer see themselves as an honest person who is in control of their life. In the past, sex addiction literature has seemed to assume that all addiction was caused by faulty core beliefs, but in my experience of working with an increasing number of opportunity-induced addictions, the feelings of low self-worth have often been a consequence of the behaviour, not the cause. However, few of us will have grown up without at least a few nagging self-doubts, and for the opportunity-induced addict, it is those doubts that the addiction resurrects.

As a society we don't generally talk about 'core beliefs' but instead focus on the impact of those beliefs on our self-esteem. If you ask someone about their self-esteem, many will at first say it is good but often what they're referring to is self-confidence. Self-confidence is the term we use to describe how we feel about the things that we 'do,' whereas self-esteem is how we feel about who we 'are.' There are many people in the world with low self-esteem who have, nonetheless, gone on to have successful careers and build beautiful homes and families. Indeed becoming good at 'doing' can become a substitute for feeling good about who you are as a person. And a life focused on creating an external image that is respected, admired and perhaps coveted by others, may be used as a cover-up for internal feelings of inadequacy.

Before we can start changing faulty core beliefs, we need to recognise what they are. Below is an exercise that can be helpful to complete to identify the most common ones.

	Often feel	Occasionally feel	Never feel
1 I'm a bad person			
2 I'm worthless			
3 I'm unimportant			
4 I'm irrelevant			
5 I'm unlovable			
6 I'm shallow			
7 I'm unwanted			
8 I'm stupid			
9 I'm foolish			
10 I'm weak			
11 I'm useless			
12 I'm a freak			
13 I'm faulty			
14 I'm a mistake			
15 I'm needy			
16 I'm greedy			

If you have ticked 'often' for any of these statements or have ticked so many statements 'occasionally' that they add up to often feeling bad about yourself, then you're probably experiencing shame.

Shame

Thaddeus Birchard writes eloquently about shame describing it as "'an awful feeling arising from a belief that you are inherently and intrinsically defective'" (Birchard, 2017: 27) and goes on to explain how shame leads people to try and hide their brokenness from others through withdrawal or attack, and from themselves with self-blame and perfectionism. Shame is perhaps one of the most painful emotions we can experience and consequently it perpetuates the cycle of addiction as a person acts out to alleviate the pain of shame only to find it creates more. While someone is trapped in shame, recovery is not possible and relapse is almost inevitable.

It's important to distinguish between shame and guilt. Shame can be described as a painfully negative emotion where the self is seen as bad and unworthy, whereas guilt is a negative judgement about a behaviour. Hence guilt says 'I have done something bad' whereas shame says 'I am bad.' Both have a long tradition as both causes and consequences of addiction but research has shown that whereas shame is likely to increase addictive behaviour, guilt can be a significant motivator to overcome it (Gilliland et al., 2011).

The links specifically between shame and sex addiction have been widely written about (Dhuffar et al., 2017), and contrary to the belief of some, the shame experienced by people with sex addiction is rarely from any ethical or anti-sex perspective. On the contrary, most of the clients I work with have no moral objection to watching pornography or visiting sex workers. Their shame comes from prioritising these activities over and above their commitments to partners, children, friends, work, finances, health and career and personal development. Furthermore, their experience of shame is deep rooted and goes back to childhood experiences that created their faulty core beliefs, rather than simply being linked to their current behaviours.

To overcome any addiction, the behaviour must be empathically explored to ensure that faulty core beliefs are not reinforced which would lead to greater feelings of shame. As shame reduces, there is then freedom to either decide that perhaps the behaviour is not a problem in itself, or, by reframing shame to guilt, a client can feel more empowered to change. What's more, with a healthy set of core beliefs, it's easier to believe that addiction can be overcome and a new life can be enjoyed, which means that commitment to recovery is a positive choice rather than an enforced obligation.

Changing core beliefs

The first approach to changing faulty core beliefs is simply to challenge their truth and reality. Motivational Interviewing techniques can be particularly useful for highlighting discrepancies in the belief – for example, noticing the times and circumstances when you are a good person or highlighting the ways you've succeeded and are loved. Cognitive behavioural therapy can also be used to establish change through exercises such as writing a cost/benefit analysis of maintaining a negative belief or writing flash cards of new positive beliefs along with the evidence to support it. I find Transactional Analysis a useful tool, too, as it is often the internal ego state of the Critical Parent that is keeping the negative belief alive. When someone is able to move to their Adult ego state they often find it easier to rationally challenge the belief and re-write it. Another strategy is to use techniques from ACT, (Acceptance and Commitment Therapy). ACT differs from CBT by focussing on accepting and defusing negative thoughts rather than challenging them. Using skills such as mindfulness, ACT encourages us to notice the thoughts and feelings we experience and feel empowered to take appropriate, value based decisions about how to respond to them and commit to positive action. For more information on these strategies, do take a look at the further reading section at the end of this book.

Whilst some faulty core beliefs, once brought into conscious awareness, can be quickly rectified, those that are deeply linked to unresolved psychological issues, as explored in Chapter 3, may require longer-term therapy. And until these causes of sex or porn addiction are dealt with, an anaesthetic will still be sought. If someone has a complex trauma and attachment-induced addiction, then it may take years of therapy to resolve the underlying problem – we explore this further in Chapter 12. Although a cognitive understanding of the problem may have been reached, this knowledge takes time to filter into emotions and behaviour. And unfortunately the nature of the cycle of addiction is that each relapse may reinforce negative core beliefs and hence create more triggers and more acting out.

Reducing shame

Reducing shame is one of the toughest therapeutic challenges in treating both sex and porn addiction and is an ongoing process throughout the work. Shame thrives in secrecy and it is often not until shame is brought into the light that it can be truly dealt with. Many people with addiction will not initially be aware of their shame as their addiction has successfully anaesthetised it, but as the anaesthetic wears off in recovery, it will become more and more apparent. A common strategy for managing shame is grandiosity, which can make it particularly difficult for a therapist and those close to the addict to recognise the problem and empathise with him or her.

Shame can be particularly hard to work with in individual therapy. No matter how much genuine support, empathy and acceptance is offered, there's no getting around the fact that 'it's a therapist's job' to make a client feel better. Hence, the reassurance may not be received. And ironically, the stronger the therapeutic alliance between client and therapist, the more a client may feel like a failure or a disappointment if they are not making adequate progress or must confess to another relapse. These feelings are often a projection from childhood or from a couple relationship but, nonetheless, they can fuel shame. In addition, a therapist may often find themselves in a 'one step forward, two steps back' dilemma, as each shame-reducing intervention is countered by shame-inducing messages and events outside of the therapy room, for example, hurtful comments from an angry or betrayed partner, or the shame experienced by seeing how a much-loved partner has been broken by the discovery. Others who know about the behaviour, such as family members or work colleagues, may belittle and deride and the latest media headline about perverts or love rats can pierce deep. There may be ongoing negative consequences even after acting out has ended, such as STIs, financial problems, or unemployment, that continually fuel shame, and if there's a slip or relapse, all the other sources of shame are disproportionally compounded.

Ultimately shame can only be reduced by connection with others. The relationship between therapist and client, especially where an integrative relational psychotherapy approach is used, can undoubtedly begin to reduce shame and repair attachment wounds, but nothing can compete with the love and acceptance of peers. Shame withers when others value us, in spite of our vulnerabilities and failures, and that is why group work and the 12-Steps are so important for addiction recovery. What's more, many people who've struggled with addiction are reluctant to let go of their shame, as they believe it to be part of their penance, or proof that they've accepted responsibility. Many also falsely believe that continuing shame is a necessary reminder of the pain they've caused which will help them not to act out again.

Like addiction, shame is a choice, and no one has to live with shame. When we connect with others, we can begin to let go of shame. We will explore the many different ways connection builds recovery in Chapter 14, but first, let's take a look at how the recovered life may look.

References

Birchard, T.B. (2017) *Overcoming Sex Addiction: A Self-Help Guide*, Routledge, London.

Carnes, P. (2001) *Out of the Shadows*, Hazelden, Center City, MN.

Dhuffar, M.K., & Griffiths, M.D. (2017) The role of shame in sexual addiction, a review of empirical research, in Birchard, T., Benfield, J. (eds) *The Routledge International Handbook of Sexual Addiction*, Routledge, London: pages 144–153.

Gilliland, R.D., South, M., Carpenter, B., & Hardy, S. (2011) The roles of shame and guilt in hypersexual behaviour, *Sexual Addiction & Compulsivity*, 18: 12–29.

11 The C.H.O.I.C.E. recovery model
Have a vision

There are two ways of looking at addiction recovery, either you can see it as giving something up, or you can see it as starting something new. Both are of course true, but it's your choice whether to focus on the losses or the gains: on the past or on the future. Committing to recovery requires changing negative core beliefs and developing a vision of a new, happier future; a future that is free of shame and offers fulfilment. Inevitably there will be a mourning period for what has been lost, but as long as there is true hope for the future, the loss process can be made bearable.

In this chapter we will be exploring how to create a vision for life that will replace the addiction and provide motivation for change, even when recovery feels tough. And we'll look at how to build a lifestyle that fits with your vision and use goal setting to maintain commitment and motivation. But first we need to look at values, as a vision that is not cemented in a personal value system will feel shallow and meaningless and be quickly forgotten.

Establishing your values

Values can be defined as the principles in our life from which we derive meaning and fulfilment and it's something we tend to hold on to very early. They form our belief system that tells us what is right and wrong so when we live a life that is in line with our personal values, we are able to feel good about ourselves. Those values can also be used to determine our priorities and our decision-making. In every case that I have worked with, sex addiction contradicts the personal value system of the individual, leaving them feeling ashamed and out of control. Over time, personal values slowly erode and many people may have forgotten what's really important to them. As part of the survey (Hall, 2013), I asked 'In what way has your sex addiction contradicted your personal value system?' Here is what just a few people said:-

'It made me a hypocrite. Everything I brought my children up to believe in I was doing the opposite.'

'I feel and think like a bully sometimes ... but I hate bullies!'

'I believe in monogamy and fidelity. I would never intentionally have hurt my partner. However my sexual acting out completely contradicts this.'

'It's totally the opposite to the real me. It's like there is a part of me that relentlessly demands satisfaction causing absolute inner turmoil and conflict with the real me. Or is this real me? That's the thought that destroys my self esteem and eats the soul.'

'I consider myself generally as a caring, sensitive person for whom family means everything and I believe everyone should be treated with honesty and respect, yet I have abused the trust my wife had in me through repeatedly lying and continuing with my addictive behaviour.'

'It makes me question my capability to be a mother and a good friend.'

'I don't believe in hurting women. But my behaviour is contributing to the exploitation of women, isn't it? Somewhere along the line someone is getting hurt aren't they? Even if I don't see it. I'm not happy that I'm cheating on my partner either.'

'I probably would dislike and disapprove of me if I met me.'

'I devalue myself. I destroy the gifts of my life. I hurt others.'

'My addiction could only survive within a bubble of lies and deceit, which to someone who thinks of himself as an honest and truthful person is a complete contradiction of values.'

'I feel ashamed of violating my values ... I am dirty and unworthy. I failed myself and feel sad ... I thought I could never wipe the slate clean.'

'I believe in life and in creativity and love. Sex addiction kills all of that and leaves you spiritually, morally, emotionally, mentally and physically dead. You're like a living junkie, only the scars are hidden inside you – no one else can see.'

'I believed I was a moral person but I did the most immoral things.'

'I always thought of myself as an honest and kind person. My addiction and the behaviours required to maintain it have made me a liar, a pervert and someone who has hurt the ones I love more than I ever thought possible.'

By reclaiming and recommitting to our personal value system, we can get back in touch with the things that give meaning and purpose to life. What's more, living a life based on values is a fundamental to the principles of 12-Step programmes to ensure that healthy choices are made. What follows is an exercise to help consider some common personal values. The list is by no means exhaustive so working through it may trigger additional values that are of more importance. In my practice I recommend that clients tick the 10 or more values that are most important to them and then put them in order of importance and priority.

Value List

Living with integrity
Living with compassion
Sharing my true self with others
Strengthening my role as a partner
Strengthening my role as a parent
Being an inspiration to others
Showing appreciation to others
Being dedicated to my work
Being charitable and generous
Developing intellectual depth
Expressing my spirituality
Being dependable
Being honest and trustworthy
Being considerate of others
Loving others
Being loved by others

Developing emotional maturity
Developing and enjoying creativity
Developing sustained friendships
Being validated by others
Developing patience
Connecting to my own feelings
Appreciating natural beauty/nature
Connecting to purpose and meaning
Having personal independence
Feeling in control
Being faithful
Taking care of others in need
Treating others with respect
Being financially secure
Being courageous
Acting with honour and being honourable

Value based decision-making

We all have to make decisions in our life, some are every day easy ones, such as 'what shall I have for lunch?' Others are more complicated, such as 'do I need a new car?' and others are really difficult, such as 'should we invite an aging parent to live with us?' Almost every decision we make in life is influenced by our emotions and most will have an impact on others. No one wants to make a decision that they will later regret, though inevitably, without a crystal ball, that may sometimes happen, but when we make decisions based on our values, rather than on our emotions, we're far more likely to be able live with the outcome.

People with addictions tend to make decisions based on emotions; based on how they feel, rather than based on the values they believe in. That often includes lying to avoid discovery or create opportunities to act out, coercing others into sexual behaviours, being unfaithful to a loved partner or watching porn rather than focussing on work or studies. The end result is almost inevitably feelings of shame and regret, as well as escalation of behaviours and a further eroding of the value system. When we choose to make decisions based on our values, rather than our emotions, our values become reinforced and we can feel proud that we have 'done the right thing', even if the consequence is temporarily painful.

Establishing and living by our values is essential to our mental health as well as to our relationships with others, and key to recovering from addiction. As the French proverb says 'there is no softer pillow than a clean conscience.'

Creating a vision

Once values have been established, or re-established, the next task for securing motivation is to create a vision for the future, a future that will replace the addiction and bring a sense of integrity and well-being. In my clinical experience creating a vision can cement a commitment to recovery more than anything else and can literally be life changing.

There are a number of different ways to consider what our vision might be, and most are based on looking squarely at our human mortality and the inevitability of death. When we acknowledge that we really do have just a finite time on this earth and we have no idea how long that will be, it can be a motivator to ensure we spend that time wisely. There's a story of a man who heroically risked his life to save a teenage boy from drowning. Once safely on shore the teenager said 'Thank you for saving my life;' the man's response was 'You're welcome, just make sure it's a life worth saving!'

Writing a vision

One effective way of writing a vision is to write your own eulogy. A depressing thought perhaps, but we are all going to die and have a funeral and most of us hope that there will be people at the funeral who will miss us. This exercise involves thinking of one or two people in your life today who may have the responsibility of standing up at your funeral to share their personal reflections and memories of their time with you. You might choose a friend, a partner, a parent, a close colleague or a child. Take a sheet of paper and write what you hope they would say. What do you want their main memories of you to be? That you were fun? Interesting? Caring? Loyal? Generous? What achievements of yours do you hope they'll remember? What would they say you enjoyed most about life? What would they say you were proudest about? What lessons would they say that you had taught them? How would they say that you had enriched their life? What will they say they will miss most? If you're struggling to do this because you don't feel proud of yourself or don't feel you've achieved anything, then think about what those things might be and it can become part of your vision to achieve them.

Once you've completed this, take a look at each of the eulogies you've written and combine them into one document. But everywhere you've written 'he/she was' write 'I will be' – for example, if you wrote 'he was kind and caring and he enjoyed making others laugh,' you'll write 'I will be kind and caring and enjoy making others laugh,' or 'he was proud of his career and taught me how to follow my dreams,' you'll write, 'I will be proud of my career and encourage others to follow their dreams.'

Creating a vision is just the start. A decision must then be made to intentionally live a life that pursues that vision. To turn the vision into achievable goals and give those goals the same level of passion and intensity that the addiction had previously consumed. The next task is to look at your current lifestyle and see how it matches up to your vision.

Evaluating your lifestyle

The great writer and social activist Thomas Merton said: 'Happiness is not a matter of intensity, but of balance and order and rhythm and harmony.' Most people with sex addiction have relied on intensity to provide a sense of happiness, and in recovery the challenge is to find happiness within a balanced life. When our lives are in balance it is easier to maintain an emotional equilibrium. That's not to say there won't be times of extreme pleasure and extreme pain, but when a life is balanced we're better able to manage, or avoid, polarities of emotion. A balanced life is also a life that is rich with variety and focuses on the needs of every aspect of being human.

There are a number of different opinions on what constitutes a balanced life, but most agree it's a combination of work, rest and play – sometimes alone, sometimes with others. In my experience, a balanced life includes eight elements – relationship, friendship, family, fun, relaxation, work, personal growth and social contribution. The importance of each of these areas will vary from individual to individual and change over the course of life. To maintain balance, we must be ready to adapt when circumstances dictate, but no element should be entirely absent. We will now explore what each of these areas of life means in more depth.

1. *Relationship* – This refers to a primary couple relationship. As we saw in Chapter 5, a happy and fulfilling couple relationship can be an invaluable source of comfort and motivation in recovery. And indeed, a stable couple relationship is an important part of many people's lives. It is a well-known fact that many otherwise happy relationships fail due to lack of attention and effort, and therefore it's important to work at our couple relationships. There are of course many people who are single and some who choose to remain so, either temporarily or long term.

2. *Friends* – Friends play a variety of essential roles in our lives, which we will explore much further in Chapter 14. A close friend can be a trusted confidant, who can support you in the challenges of recovery, whilst other friends may be a source of fun and recreation. Regrettably friendship is often side-lined for the more urgent needs of work and family, but they play a key role in helping to maintain a balanced life.

3. *Family* – Nowadays, families come in many different shapes and sizes. Parents, step-parents, grandparents, step-grandparents, siblings, half-siblings, step-siblings, aunts, uncles, cousins, nieces, nephews and a whole load of other second or in-law relations. The discovery, or disclosure, of addiction may highlight problems that have been around for many years, or may reveal a depth of understanding and support that had hitherto gone unnoticed or been taken for granted. Either way, family in whatever way you define it, or experience it, is an inevitable part of life that can be maximised for optimum reward.

4. *Fun and recreation* – When sex, or any other compulsive substance or activity, has been a part of someone's lifestyle for a long time, other pastimes often lose their appeal or disappear altogether. Play

is part of being human. From birth to old age, the desire to have fun, to laugh and be creative, is universal. In terms of Transactional Analysis, this area of life emanates from the free child. The shame of addiction often robs people of their ability to get in touch with their inner free child and innocent fun may be a dim and distant memory. Getting back in touch with this part of ourselves and giving it a place to express itself in our lifestyle is a key component of becoming whole and healthy again.

5 *Rest and relaxation* – Many activities that might be classed fun and recreational are not necessarily relaxing. While it's important to have activities that stimulate us, it's also important to have periods of time that are devoted to slowing down. Busyness seems to be a curse of 21st-century living and many people feel guilty if they're not doing something perceived as productive with their time. But relaxing is productive, because it allows us to recharge our batteries and gives space for inspiration to be born. For those who used their addiction to anaesthetise against stress and anxiety, learning new ways to relax is especially important.

6 *Work* – Another area of our lives that can give satisfaction is work – that could be voluntary work, paid employment, part time or full time. Whatever form work takes, it is a place where you have the potential to feel good about what you give and produce, and what you receive in terms of financial and/or emotional reward. Unfortunately work can also be a significant trigger for some people with addiction, either due to the opportunity it provides to act out, or because of the negative emotions it creates. When work is a problem area, ideally energy should be focused on improving the current situation or changing career, but if that's not possible, expanding in other areas of life can make an unsatisfactory job more tolerable.

7 *Personal growth* – Where work is not a source of pleasure, it is especially important to take time to focus on personal growth. It is the nature of being human that we enjoy learning. We like to expand our knowledge and our skill set. To feel a sense of achievement that comes from personal endeavour. And since this is an area of life that is not dependent on other people, it provides an opportunity to be completely focused on personal needs and desires. Personal growth means different things to different people. For some it may be learning a new skill or being creative while for others it may mean emotional growth through therapy, or reading or mindfulness exercises; alternatively it could be spiritual growth through prayer or other religious practices. It doesn't matter what it is as long as there is a sense of self-improvement and progress.

8 *Contribution* – Contribution is perhaps the opposite of personal growth. It refers to the part of life where we give to others or give back to society. It is the place where we can develop our empathy and enjoy the rewards of altruism. When we give to others, it also allows us to step outside of ourselves and see the world from another perspective. Depending on the activity it can also provide a positive sense of agency and influence. Making a contribution may mean getting more involved in politics or social or environmental issues. It may involve working for, or contributing to a charity or helping someone nearby. Many recovering addicts, especially those in 12-Step communities, make a commitment to give back in some way to support fellow addiction sufferers.

In Figure 11.1 you'll see an illustration of a life wheel with all of these eight areas of life coming from a central point of your value system. This is a concept widely used in life coaching as a tool to discover which areas of life may need more attention. The principle is that by looking at the wheel and marking your degree of satisfaction between 1 and 10 on each axis (with 1 at the centre and 10 on the outside) you can see how balanced your life is and therefore how smoothly the wheel of life will turn. And the more high marks you're able to score yourself, the richer your life will be and the more overall satisfaction you're likely to gain from it. Please note, the rating is based

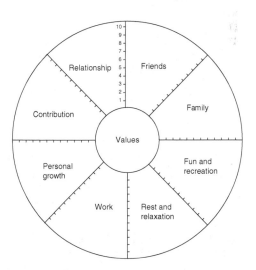

Figure 11.1 The life wheel

on personal satisfaction. Therefore, if you are single, and very happy being single, then you would score 10 on the relationship section. Completing the exercise will allow you to see how balanced your life is and therefore how smoothly the wheel of life will turn.

Any addiction can quickly become part of someone's lifestyle and some struggle to imagine a life without it. For long-term recovery to be successful, that lifestyle has to change. Completing the life wheel should have provided valuable information about the areas of life where change is both desired and required. Now it's time to set some goals to make the wheel bigger and more even.

Setting goals

Talking to clients about setting goals gets a mixed reaction. Some groan at what sounds like hard and tedious work, while others become excited at the prospect of having a formal plan of action. Whatever the reaction, goal setting is a key element of addiction recovery and can provide structure to the process as well as a way of evaluating success and maintaining motivation. To ensure that goal setting is effective and pleasurable they need to be positively framed. This means that they are written as a benefit. For example, rather than setting a goal of dieting to lose 10 lbs, it would be written as achieving a target weight or getting to a certain waist size. Goals also need to be S.M.A.R.T. – Specific, Measurable, Attainable, Relevant and Time-related – we will look at each of these in turn now:

- *Specific* – what exactly do you want to achieve? For example, rather than 'earn more money' – how much more? Or 'take up a new sport?' – which sport?
- *Measurable* – what evidence will you see to know that you've achieved your goal, for example a goal that is 'to eat healthier' would be better written as 'eat 5 pieces of fruit or portions of vegetables a day.'
- *Attainable* – for goals to be effective and motivating, they need to be attainable. In other words, you need the resources and time to achieve them and they need to be wholly within your control. Hence 'make my partner trust me' should be written as 'become accountable to my partner.'
- *Relevant* – this means ensuring goals are relevant to what you want to achieve, and in terms of recovery that means they're goals that will lead to a better lifestyle that is in line with your values and vision.

- *Time-related* – this means having a deadline to achieve the goal by, or a time-scale for an activity. For example, rather than 'go to 12-Step meetings' it would be 'go to at least two meetings a month starting next month.'

In our recovery groups we recommend setting SMART goals that will expand the life wheel just one increment at a time to ensure there is measurable progress which will build motivation and commitment to recovery. Hence someone who only scored themselves two for satisfaction on friends will aim for three, rather than trying to get straight to ten. As each goal is reached another can be set to further the recovery journey and establish a positive and satisfying lifestyle as an alternative to the addiction.

With values re-established and a vision of life without addiction in place, along with some SMART goals for how to achieve it, hopefully there is now sufficient motivation to overcome the compulsive behaviours and start living a life of choice, rather than one governed by addiction.

References

Hall, P. (2013) *Understanding and Treating Sex Addiction*, Routledge, London.

12 The C.H.O.I.C.E. recovery model
Overcome compulsive behaviours

It may seem strange to some readers that this is not the first step in recovery, but in my experience many people with addiction struggle to stop acting out until they've confronted any self-limiting core beliefs and have developed a vision for the future. Without doing so, many find themselves confronted with feelings of loss and regret rather than hope and optimism. What's more, putting future first helps to reinforce the fact that abstinence is not the same as recovery and the decision to stop acting out has come from a place of positive choice rather than fatalistic resignation. Having said that, this is the longest chapter in the book and includes exercises that will help develop a deeper understanding of what causes and maintains the addiction as well strategies for stopping unwanted behaviours.

In order to overcome compulsive behaviours it's essential that each person understands their individual cycle of addiction and the unique factors that keep them trapped in their behaviour. Back in Chapter 4, I introduced you to the six-phase model that I use in my recovery courses and here we will explore that cycle in more depth. By going into each phase of the cycle and identifying the individual thoughts, feelings and behaviours that happen at each point, it becomes possible to establish ways to break the cycle.

For example, someone with a trauma-induced addiction might identify that feelings of anxiety 'trigger' acting out – once discovered, work can begin in therapy to find healthier ways to manage anxiety alongside making lifestyle changes that reduce it. Someone with a pure opportunity-induced addiction might identify that one of the cognitive distortions they use within the preparation phase is telling themselves 'I can't masturbate without pornography.' Having identified this they can then learn mindful masturbation in addition to establishing if sexual desire is the motivator or another emotional need. An attachment-induced addict may recognise that during the regret phase, when they feel huge guilt at betraying their partner, this impacts them in the reconstitution phase as they find themselves being compliant to unreasonable demands rather than addressing underlying relationship issues.

As explained previously, each phase of the cycle is unique to each individual and will last for differing amounts of time depending on the person and on the circumstances. Some may spend months in the dormant phase while for others it may only be days. Others will spend weeks in preparation and for others it will be minutes. It's also important to note that the lines are blurred between each phase. Identifying exactly when the dormant phase has ended with a trigger or developed into preparation is almost impossible but fortunately it's not important. As long as the key features of the cycle are identified (see Figure 12.1), knowing precisely when they happen isn't significant.

Over the following pages of this chapter I will offer a number of tools and evaluation exercises that can be used either alone or in a treatment setting to begin to identify the individual components of the addiction cycle. It doesn't matter whereabouts on the cycle you start, since the very nature of a cycle means it has no real beginning or end. Therefore it's usually easiest to start with a phase that seems the simplest to answer or is more consciously available. Most people find that a pattern soon begins to build as they work round. For example, having completed the exercises for the dormant phase and identified that 'loneliness' is particularly difficult to manage and the quality of relationships is inadequate, it will then become easier to recognise that feeling lonely and being rejected by a partner is a common trigger.

Throughout this chapter we will use Craig as a case example and see how he completed his personalised cycle.

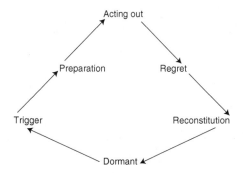

Figure 12.1 The six-phase cycle of addiction

> **Craig**
>
> Craig is a 24-year-old who has struggled with pornography addiction and escalated use of webcam sex for nearly ten years. He always assumed he would stop when he met the 'right' girl but now, in spite of being two years into a loving relationship, the problem is still there. His addiction was primarily opportunity-induced with some attachment issues too.

The dormant phase

The dormant phase of the addiction cycle is where the addiction may appear to be temporarily in remission and life has returned to 'normal.' But 'normal' for someone with an addiction is a place where underlying needs continue to be unmet and issues relating to opportunity, trauma and attachment remain unresolved. Assuming you've already completed the core belief exercise in Chapter 10 and the life wheel in Chapter 11, you may have already identified areas of your life that you know you need to work on. The following exercise can further help you to consider how well you manage emotionally on a day-to-day basis and the primary feelings that your addiction may help you to escape.

Evaluating emotional regulation

How good are you at 'healthily' managing the following feelings?

	Good	Average	Poor
Loneliness			
Feeling I don't belong			
Boredom			
Sadness			
Anxiety			
Anger and frustration			
Stress			
Feeling overwhelmed			
Shame			

	Good	Average	Poor
Rejection			
Unfairness			
Sexual frustration			

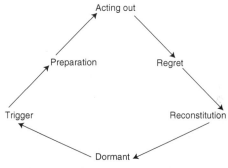

Feelings: Loneliness, boredom, shame, frustration

Figure 12.2 Craig's cycle

The trigger phase

Some people recognise one or two common triggers that propel them out of dormancy towards acting out. But for many others there are a series of triggers, each quietly building upon the other until sufficient momentum is built to go into the preparation phase.

Identifying triggers is a crucial part of addiction recovery since without it, it's impossible to learn how to avoid and/or manage those triggers. However, some people may struggle to identify triggers until there's been a period of abstinence because they experience their behaviour as being 'habit.' When an opportunity arises, such as being alone in the house or away on a business trip, acting out is something they automatically do because they always have. Although this is undoubtedly true, and indeed there's some neurological basis for this (Voon, 2014), making note of those trigger environments may uncover hidden issues and will enable successful relapse prevention techniques to be developed. The exercise in Box 12.1 can be used to identify triggers.

Box 12.1 Identifying triggers

Opportunity related triggers

These are the triggers that are most likely to occur for each category of addiction and relate to lifestyle and general emotional management. Tick as many as appropriate.

Environmental

- Empty house ☐
- Unprotected Internet ☐
- Having time on your hands ☐
- Having money in your pocket ☐
- Being abroad ☐
- Being in cities or certain place ☐
- Being away from home ☐
- Seeing an attractive person ☐
- Being flattered or flirted with ☐
- Being with certain people ☐
- When using alcohol or drugs ☐
- When you've achieved something ☐
- When you've got a hangover ☐
- Other ☐

Emotional

- Feeling bored ☐
- Feeling stressed ☐
- Feeling angry ☐
- Feeling sorry for yourself ☐
- Feeling ill or tired ☐
- Feeling unfulfilled ☐
- Feeling entitled ☐
- Feeling ashamed ☐
- Feeling sexually aroused ☐
- Feeling exhilarated ☐
- Feeling worthless ☐
- Feeling omnipotent ☐
- Feeling guilty ☐
- Loss of self esteem ☐
- Other ☐

Attachment related triggers

Someone with an Attachment Induced addiction is likely to identify with many of the following triggers that all relate to feelings generated within relationship to others. Tick as many as appropriate.

Getting into an argument with a loved one ☐
Feeling overwhelmed by responsibility and/or duty ☐
Feeling trapped by another's needs ☐
Feeling unable to confront a loved one ☐
Feeling unable to communicate your needs and/or views ☐
Not having enough time for yourself ☐
Feeling rejected ☐
Feeling lonely ☐
Feeling left out ☐
Feeling unvalued ☐
Feeling unloved ☐
Feeling attacked and/or defensive ☐

Other _____

Trauma related triggers

These triggers will be most relevant to those with a Trauma Induced addiction and connect to how stress and anxiety are managed. Tick as many as appropriate.

When life is particularly stressful ☐
When life feels out of control ☐
When life feels empty and meaningless ☐
Feeling fearful ☐
Feeling powerless ☐
Feeling anxious ☐
Feeling depressed ☐
Feeling empty or dead inside ☐
Feeling agitated and restless ☐
When you feel vulnerable ☐
When you feel you must be strong and/or fight ☐
When your body feels tense ☐
When your body feels numb ☐

Other _____

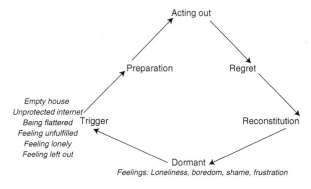

Figure 12.3 Craig's cycle

The preparation phase

Once a trigger, or series of triggers, has been experienced, someone with an addiction moves into the preparation phase where the emotions they wish to anaesthetise against gradually begin to disappear amidst the practical and psychological activities of preparing to act out. These preparations may be both conscious and unconscious but by making them fully conscious the work can then begin on stopping the cycle by eliminating them.

As discussed in Chapter 4, the activities of the preparation phase broadly fall under the headings of cognitive distortions (CDs) and SUDS. The exercises in Box 12.2 can help identify these.

Box 12.2 Recognising cognitive distortions

Below is a list of the 13 most common cognitive distortions that allow the addiction cycle to continue. Read the examples and then write down the thinking pattern that you most commonly use.

1 Rationalisation – this is when you make excuses for your behaviour using logic and reason. For example, 'Acting out is ok because I haven't done it for ages which proves it isn't an addiction' or 'It's not possible to masturbate without pornography.'

Your thinking _____

---

2 Justification – when you use excuses to defend your behaviour. For example, 'I can't help it when I'm drunk' or 'No one could resist acting out when it's handed to them on a plate.'

Your thinking _____

3 Minimisation – this is a thinking strategy for not taking full responsibility for your behaviour or staying in denial. For example, 'I'll only be online for 10 minutes' or 'It's not as bad as …'

Your thinking _____

4 Magnifying – this is the opposite of minimisation so rather than making light of something, an event or circumstance that is relatively unimportant is given greater status. For example, 'I have had an absolutely horrendous day and I am so stressed that I cannot cope so I need to act out' or 'My partner has ridiculed and abused me and therefore it's ok for me to soothe how I feel.'

Your thinking _____

5 Blame – this is when someone else is blamed for your behaviour. For example, 'If my wife was more into sex I wouldn't need to do this' or 'If my work was more fulfilling I wouldn't act out.'

Your thinking _____

6 Entitlement – this kind of thinking often comes either from grandiosity or from self-pity and is when you find reasons to tell yourself you deserve to act out. For example 'I need to act out because I didn't have much sexual experience when I was younger' or 'I work extremely hard to support my family and deserve the occasional treat.'

Your thinking _____

7 Uniqueness – this is similar to entitlement but is more about focusing on what you perceive as being unique about yourself or about your personal circumstances. For example, 'I'm a very successful person and people would expect me to enjoy sexual variety' or 'I was born with a particular fetish and this is the only way to satisfy it.'

Your thinking _____

8 Mental Filter – this strategy is used to filter out any thoughts that might stop acting out from happening. For example, 'Last time I acted out was fantastic and I didn't have any

regrets' or 'My partner is totally unreasonable all the time and so I need to act out.'

Your thinking _____

9 Victim stance – this is when you make excuses for your behaviour by putting yourself in the role of victim. For example, 'It's not my fault I act out, I was abused as a child' or 'I have to act out when everyone is picking on me.'

Your thinking _____

10 Normalisation – this is often used with generalisation to make acting out seem like 'the norm.' For example, 'All men look at pornography' or 'It's instinctive to want to sleep with a beautiful woman.'

Your thinking _____

11 Denial – this is perhaps the most common cognitive distortion and simply involves blocking out reality. For example, 'If my partner never finds out there will be no problem' or 'There is nothing wrong with acting out.'

Your thinking _____

12 Helplessness – this can be a particularly powerful cognitive distortion, especially for those with low self-esteem. For example: 'I can't help acting out, I have never had any will power' or 'I can't help it, I'm a sex addict.'

Your thinking _____

13 Invincibility – this refers to the times when you think you're 'bullet proof.' In other words 'I won't ever get caught,' 'no-one will ever know what I do' or 'I won't catch an STI.'

Your thinking _____

Identifying SUDs

Many clients have said that identifying their SUDs (seemingly unimportant decisions) has been a key element of their recovery. Even when they've not been able to identify many triggers or cognitive distortions, they have been able to recognise their behavioural actions and by bringing these into conscious awareness they are then better able to stop them.

One of the most effective ways of identifying SUDs is to create what's known as a behaviour chain. This involves thinking about the last time you acted out, or the last few times if they were very different, and working backwards to identify the events that led up to it. Box 12.3 is an example of Craig's behaviour chain.

> **Box 12.3 Identifying SUDs**
>
> Acting out event: Monday – masturbated to live web sex show
>
> - I was checking out which girls were live on the web sex site, but told myself I was only looking out of curiosity
> - I felt really stressed and decided 10 minutes of porn would help me calm down and get to sleep
> - I was looking at jobs online that I wish I was qualified to do
> - I didn't go to bed with my girlfriend because I said I was too stressed to sleep and was going to go online to look at jobs
> - I was moody all evening and pissed off about work
> - I had a really bad day at work and drove home stressing about how much I hate my job and deserve better.
>
> If this exercise is repeated over a number of acting-out events, then a pattern soon begins to emerge. For example, another client who had a problem with sleeping with sex workers noticed that the start of his behaviour chain was almost always making a decision to have a meeting in London rather than at another location. Inevitably this resulted in him telling his wife there was a social after the meeting and surreptitiously putting cash aside to pay for his behaviour.

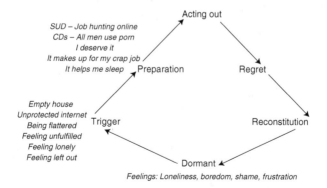

Figure 12.4 Craig's cycle

The acting out phase

The acting out phase of the addiction cycle always serves multiple functions. The most obvious ones are sexual arousal, stimulation and usually satiation, but there are emotional outcomes as well. By identifying these it becomes easier to understand which deeper needs are being satisfied and then work can begin on finding healthier ways of meeting those needs.

The exercise in Box 12.4 provides an opportunity to analyse what is gained by acting out and therefore what the additional functions of the addiction may be.

Please note that while most people experience many negative emotions such as shame and guilt as a result of their behaviour, the purpose of this exercise is to identify the positive feelings that the behaviour elicits.

The regret phase

Both the regret and the reconstitution phases of the cycle provide the opportunity for the true cost of sex and porn addiction to be realised. During the other phases, it may be easier to forget or minimise the negative consequences, but now they can hit hard. Having said that, some people experience little regret, especially if they're able to minimise or avoid the harmful effects, while others find themselves racked with guilt and shame. The regret phase may

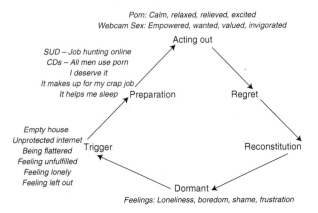

Figure 12.5 Craig's cycle

Box 12.4 Identifying the positives of acting out

Table 12.1 Emotions experienced

List acting out behaviours along here adding more space if required						
Emotions experienced	Powerful					
	Affirmed					
	Wanted					
	Valued					
	Accepted					
	Desired					
	Calm					
	Relaxed					
	Numb					
	Excited					
	Cared for					
	Connected					
	Invigorated					
	Creative					
	Relieved					
	Independent					
	In control					
	Free from responsibility					
	Disassociated					
	Feeling out of control					
	Risk					

140 *The C.H.O.I.C.E. recovery model*

last just a few hours or it may last for weeks or even months before someone is able to pick themselves up and move on to the reconstitution phase.

Identifying the impact of acting out on thoughts, feelings and behaviours can become a helpful disincentive to acting out again. But, as many will testify, in spite of the intense feelings of remorse, the behaviour does reoccur until the deeper causes have been resolved. Personalising this phase of the addictive cycle is perhaps the easiest since the anaesthetising behaviours have subsided and the brain now has the cognitive capacity to interpret thoughts and feelings. The exercise I use is shown in Box 12.5.

Box 12.5 Identifying regrets

After acting out, how do you feel about the following:

- Yourself?_____
- Your relationship?_____
- Your life?_____

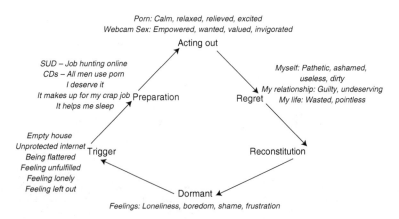

Figure 12.6 Craig's cycle

The reconstitution phase

Like the regret phase, the thoughts, emotions and events of the reconstitution phase are often easier to recognise. Some people who've been round the addiction cycle many times find themselves longing for this phase. As they go through the preparation phase they may be eager to act out, to get it over and done with, so they can begin to get their life back together and return to dormant.

The actions undertaken during this phase are almost always done with the best intention of making amends, alleviating guilt and striving to not act out again. But often they perpetuate the cycle by feeding the unmet needs. For example, someone with an attachment-induced addiction might put extra effort into not complaining about their relationship, when what they really need to do is become more assertive about their needs. And someone with a trauma-induced addiction may begin to drink more to alleviate their anxiety rather than developing healthier stress management techniques. Like the regret phase, identifying what happens during reconstitution can help someone calculate the true cost of their behaviours, and provide further motivation to change. The questions in the exercise below can help to elicit the common elements of this phase.

Box 12.6 Identifying behaviours in the reconstitution phase

After acting out, what do you do to:

- protect yourself from being discovered?
- comfort yourself emotionally?
- restore relationships with partner, family, friends?
- repair any problems created at work?
- make any necessary financial amends?
- stop yourself from acting out again?

Personalising the cycle of addiction is not a one-off task; it's a process of ongoing understanding that can continue throughout therapy and beyond. Although at the end of these exercises it's likely that someone will have a much better idea of their individual cycle, it's important to keep adding to it as new information and/or experience comes to mind.

142 The C.H.O.I.C.E. recovery model

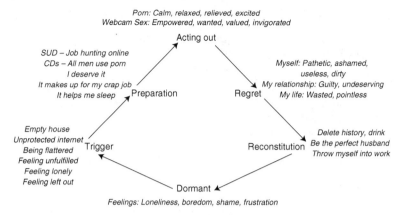

Figure 12.7 Craig's cycle

As Craig personalised his cycle he began to see how it linked to his low self-esteem and loneliness. Craig's parents had never praised him as a child and were cold and distant except on the rare occasions when he managed to meet their high academic standards. Throughout adolescence Craig worked hard to try and win his parents' approval, often to the detriment of making and maintaining friendships. He would spend hours alone in his bedroom, and whenever study got difficult, he would turn to online porn. Craig never felt good enough and as his self-esteem worsened, so his use of pornography increased. He dropped out of education completely at 16 and met his first and current girlfriend at 22. Technically he was a virgin when they first slept together, but as a connoisseur of cybersex, he hoped she wouldn't know. Now at 24 he hated his job in a call centre and struggled to believe his girlfriend really loved him as much as she said. And he was convinced she wouldn't love him if she knew about his online sex life.

Until completing his cycle of addiction, Craig had never realised his addiction was a symptom of other issues in his life. Not only did the exercise help him to highlight areas of work for therapy, but he was also able to identify where relapse prevention work needed to be focused.

Strategies for stopping the cycle

Broadly speaking there are two elements to breaking the cycle of addiction – develop comprehensive relapse prevention strategies and resolve underlying emotional and psychological issues that are maintaining the cycle. Easy to say, but regrettably somewhat harder to do. As discussed previously, many people struggle to identify underlying issues until they've managed to establish at least some level of sobriety because there may be little conscious awareness until the anaesthetic has begun to wear off. But conversely, relapse prevention strategies may be continually sabotaged by emotional triggers unless there's at least some indication of what those issues may be. In this section we are going to focus primarily on relapse prevention strategies that can quite quickly and easily be put into place and we will end this chapter exploring what further work may be required to resolve underlying issues.

Relapse prevention strategies

Within our group work programmes and individual therapy sessions we provide a wide range of strategies for stopping compulsive behaviours and we are frequently asked 'do these work?' This is, of course, a perfectly reasonable question, especially as some of the strategies appear a little strange, but the simple answer is 'yes they work if you use them.' The number one reason why relapse prevention strategies fail is when someone 'chooses' not to use them. And in therapy, when we ask 'why didn't you use one of your relapse prevention strategies,' a common explanation is 'because I knew it would work and I wanted to act out.' So as you read on, please remember that none of this will work unless you use it, and if you don't yet have the motivation, go back and read Chapters 10 and 11.

But there is another reason why relapse prevention strategies can fail and that's because people don't fully understand the power of craving. That may seem an odd thing to say, especially if you're an addict yourself, but the reality is that addicts don't know how bad craving is until they try and stop and therefore can often underestimate the psychological pain they may need to endure.

Understanding triggers and craving

As we saw previously in this chapter, broadly speaking, triggers are either environmental or emotional; and some are predictable, and therefore avoidable, whereas others can hit you like a steam train when you least expect it. Whatever the trigger, it results in the experience of craving and the longer you leave it, the greater the craving becomes. Craving can build to the extent that it dominates every other thought and feeling, it can wake you up in the middle of the night and invade your dreams when you sleep. We've talked a lot about 'choice' in this book, and regrettably, whilst you can choose not to act out, you cannot choose not to crave and acting out soon becomes a way of ending the pain of craving, rather than enjoying the drug of choice.

Furthermore, triggers are not purely psychological or emotional, they're biological. Understanding the biological component is important for understanding craving as well as for reducing disillusionment and shame. Triggers become what is known in addiction as cues that link events together and create a neurological pathway. For example, if you've had a stressful day at work and you regularly and habitually reach for a glass of wine, a neural pathway to the pleasure chemicals in your brain will gradually be created. And as you continue to reach for that glass of wine, the neural pathway becomes stronger and stronger to the point where you will unconsciously link a glass of wine to a stressful day. Similarly, if you always restock on wine when you pass a particular wine store or you always have a drink of wine when you meet a particular friend, you will soon unconsciously link both the place and the person to wine. This process is also known as classical conditioning and was famously highlighted by Pavlov's dogs. If a certain set of stimuli is continually present before a rewarding event, those stimuli become increasingly associated with the behaviour at an unconscious and neurological level.

In terms of sex and porn addiction, this means that over time the brain will have created neural pathways that respond automatically to certain triggers, with no conscious thought. For example, the sight of an attractive woman, or a day working home alone, or a business meeting in London might automatically trigger a desire to act out without any awareness of any cognitive thought. Similarly, an emotional trigger such as feeling angry, bored or lonely might instantaneously translate to sexual desire. But cues also work the opposite way around. The more you watch porn, the more you will notice attractive people and sexualise them, but the further you get into recovery, the less wired your brain will be to notice similar stimuli.

To overcome sex and porn addiction, the brain needs to re-wire. This re-wiring requires two components. First, maintaining sobriety through relapse prevention strategies to allow the unhealthy neural pathways to diminish; and second changing the emotional and cognitive response to the experience of craving.

Accepting triggers and craving

Being triggered and experiencing craving is inevitable in recovery. For some it may be felt like little more than inconvenience, especially if there's sufficient motivation for change, but, as we've seen, for some it can be psychological hell. But this hell can be made manageable by avoiding fighting it and beating yourself up about it, but instead accepting it, and making a conscious choice to do something positive. We talked about Acceptance and Commitment Therapy back in Chapter 10 and how it offers strategies for reducing the power of thoughts and cognitions. By detaching from the thought and recognising it simply as 'a thought,' it can be defused. For example, by saying 'my brain is craving to act out,' rather than 'I need to act out,' a distance is created, enabling you to make another choice. Or 'my addiction is telling me I need to look at porn to get to sleep' rather than 'I need to watch porn to sleep.' It helps us to recognise that our thoughts are 'thoughts' not facts. When this detaching technique is used alongside mindfulness and value based decision making, it forms a powerful foundation on which to build other relapse prevention strategies.

Another element of recovery that needs to be accepted is withdrawal, and when people experience withdrawal their craving will increase. Some people do not experience significant withdrawal symptoms, whilst others struggle with many. For some, the impact of withdrawal is immediate, especially for those giving up porn addiction. Common symptoms include restlessness, irritability, anxiety, depression, brain fog, lethargy, low libido, genital numbness and mood swings. Generally these fade within a month of quitting. For others, similar symptoms may appear months into recovery, though in reality, these may be an indication of underlying issues that the addiction had previously masked. Withdrawal can be uncomfortable, but it does come to an end. The strategies described in Chapter 15 for establishing confident recovery will help to reduce these symptoms, but for now we'll turn our attention to specific strategies that can be chosen to avoid triggers and/or minimise their impact.

Restrict access

First and foremost, restrict access to any acting out opportunities. For almost everyone with a sex addiction and certainly everyone with a porn addiction, that means blocking access to pornography at source and on individual devices, contacting ISPs to ensure parental controls are in place and utilising these on any other internet device. In addition, blocking software can be installed onto routers, such as OpenDNS, and onto each device, such as Netnanny or Covenant Eyes. In addition to blocking software, tracking can also be added which will send an accountability report to a designated other person on your internet use.

Whilst there's an ever-growing range of blocking options, many of which are quite sophisticated now, absolutely none of them are foolproof and a determined addict could get round any of them and even enjoy this as part of the challenge, but the more you can do to restrict your access, the more time you buy yourself to make a better choice.

Look the other way

A common problem many people have in early recovery is attractive people. They seem to be everywhere, on public transport, on the street, in restaurants, at work and on every screen you look at. It is of course natural to notice attractive people, but you choose whether to 'notice' or 'stare.' The simplest and most effective strategy is simply to look away. Many refer to what's known as the 3 second rule, counting 1, 2 then looking the other way. Other strategies include making sure you're facing the wall in public places so you're less likely to notice people or scan on the off chance.

Change your environment

Earlier in this chapter there was an opportunity to identify triggers and it's likely that quite a few environmental boxes were ticked. When it comes to triggers, the number one relapse prevention strategy, especially in early recovery, is to avoid them. This means that any places, people or activities that have provided the opportunity to act out or have served as some kind of encouragement, must be avoided, such as being in an environment where sex is easily available, as in certain districts of certain towns and cities, or being alone in the house with unrestricted access to pornography. For some, environmental triggers also include people, such as being with friends or work colleagues who regularly go to strip clubs or who talk openly about their porn use. In most circumstances, environmental triggers can be avoided, but that takes rigorous self-honesty and discipline. And it might sometimes mean letting someone else down. So if an invitation comes to a stag party in Amsterdam, the answer is no. For people struggling with porn addiction, it can be particularly helpful to change the environment of their devices and where they use them. That might mean changing passwords and pins to something encouraging, making sure there's a photo of a loved one as a screen saver or an image that represents their vision. Changing the physical room environment can also help, putting the bed or desk in a different position, changing pictures on the walls. The more you can do to interrupt the neurological cues the better. For some, the only way to avoid work-related triggers is to change job. That can be a difficult decision to make that might involve financial losses. But those losses need to be weighed up against what would be lost if the addiction is not conquered.

Manage your time

Many people with addiction feel as though they're surrounded by triggers and avoiding them is almost impossible. This is certainly true on some occasions, but the vast majority can be avoided if thought through in advance. The old cliché 'failing to prepare is preparing to fail' is particularly true in addiction and therefore a key element of relapse prevention is planning. If there are certain routines or situations that are triggering, plan ahead to avoid them. For example, if having an evening alone at home, or perhaps in a hotel, is a trigger, arrange to meet a friend, go to the cinema or take a book to read. If stress is a trigger, consider how to reduce this to a minimum, at least in the early stages of recovery. Being prepared can often minimise stress, for example by allowing more time for travel or for achieving a task, or stopping yourself from checking work email outside of work hours. Too much time and surplus cash are common triggers that can often be avoided through developing practical strategies. First get a diary or open a spreadsheet to ensure any spare time is usefully filled and made accountable. Free time not only provides opportunity for people with addictions to act out but, if not usefully used, can also be a painful experience as the urge to act out has space to grow. But with a bit of pre-planning this can be avoided, or at least minimised. Spare cash can be another strong temptation. One way to manage this is to ensure that all money is accountable between couples and that only a minimum amount of cash is ever carried around. For people who are single, it can be helpful to ensure that any excess funds that are not required for daily living are put into a savings account that is hard to access.

R.U.N.

Unfortunately, some triggers are unavoidable. For many people, seeing an attractive woman or sexual image on the street or in the media, being flirted with or being confronted with an easy opportunity, such as an unprotected PC or unexpected time alone, can be especially difficult to negotiate

There is one very practical, and highly successful strategy that can be employed here and that is R.U.N. Quite literally this means get out of the situation, and get out fast. Whether that means leaving the house, the office, the hotel or whatever it is, Get away from the opportunity immediately. In addition, it can be a useful acrostic to remember:

- **R**emove yourself immediately from the situation – don't let yourself flirt with temptation for even a second more than you have to – get out now.
- **U**ndistort your thinking – this will not make you feel better, one more time does matter, you do not deserve this, you do not want to have to lie again.
- **N**ever forget what you have to lose – you made the decision to stop acting out because it was ruining your life – that fact has not changed.

Learning to R.U.N. is perhaps the single most important relapse prevention technique there is. I have heard countless stories of relapse when this simple principle went unheeded. If a trigger is ignored, minimised, flirted with or indulged, it will become stronger and stronger. Immediate action is always the best policy.

Short, sharp shocks

There are very few situations when RUNning is impossible, but if you do find yourself in one of them, such as looking after sleeping children, or stuck at a boring desk job, there are a number of other techniques that can be helpful for beating unavoidable triggers. Remember earlier I said there were some techniques that were a bit strange – here they come! Craving is often experienced as an almost trance like state where rational thinking and feeling goes out of the window and one of the most effective ways of breaking that trance is through a physical shock. A cold shower is the most obvious one, but if that's not possible, suck on an ice cube, or hold an ice cube to the roof of your mouth to give yourself brain freeze. Other strategies that have helped are sucking a lemon, biting into a chilli, or sniffing smelling salts. The objective is to jolt your body back into the reality of the current moment. A less painful alternative, which can also be very effective, is to look at yourself in a mirror. This may sound very simplistic, but looking deeply into your own eyes, saying your name and 'is this what I really want' can work as a powerful wake-up call.

Distraction

Distraction is undoubtedly a useful technique, but it only works when it's part of a wider strategy of recovery, such as C.H.O.I.C.E. and/or 12-Step. Distraction alone does not result in long-term recovery, but it can be a powerful way of minimising craving, especially when used with the R.U.N. acrostic. It's believed that most cravings last between 15 and 20 minutes. Therefore, having a list of things to preoccupy yourself with will make the craving easier to endure. Distractions might include physical exercise or yoga or mindfulness; watching a TED talk or a favourite TV programme or comedy sketch; listening to music, a radio programme, or a podcast; playing a game such as Sudoku or tetras or a mind game; elephoning a friend or family member or simply going out in a public place such as a park or supermarket. It doesn't matter what you do as long as it takes you away from the stimuli and somewhere else.

Distraction should not be confused with positive recovery habits, which we'll look at more in Chapter 15, as the point is to escape thoughts of the addiction. Therefore techniques such as podcasts or TED talks should not be recovery based and it's probably best not to telephone someone else in recovery, unless you know you can talk to them about something else. This principle is based on NLP (Neuro Linguistic Programming). If you don't want to think about lemons, don't say 'don't think about lemons,' but rather 'think about oranges.' So if you're trying not to think about addiction and acting out, make sure you're thinking about something completely unrelated. Once the craving has passed and the trigger has lost its momentum, then is the time to engage in recovery activities and connect with others for support – there is much more about this in the following chapters.

Although triggers can be painful and difficult to manage, it's important to recognise that they can provide essential clues to the underlying function of the addiction. Furthermore, successfully managing triggers can create positive self-esteem and deepen commitment to recovery. Someone who has never been tempted often has less self-confidence than someone who has survived temptation.

As stated at the beginning of this section, relapse prevention strategies do not work unless you 'use' them, but there is more to recovery than simply stopping acting out. A life of avoiding triggers and RUNning, is not real life. True recovery means developing a healthy and fulfilling lifestyle where the compulsive behaviours are no longer needed and in addition to Connecting to Others (Chapter 14) and Establishing Confident Recovery (Chapter 15) that also means getting to the root of the problem and digging it out.

Resolving underlying issues

Back in Chapter 10 we explored the most common faulty core beliefs that not only cause compulsive behaviours, but also maintain the cycle of addiction. Most of these will have developed during childhood and whilst CBT and ACT techniques may help to reduce them, most people need to dig deeper to remove them altogether. All addictions serve the function of controlling emotion. For example, some recreational drug users take drugs to create a positive emotion of euphoria, while others use their drug of choice to anaesthetise against negative feelings. Or of course, many do both. The same is true of sex and porn addiction. Hence engaging in cyber sex or having multiple affairs may create a positive emotion of feeling wanted and affirmed, while losing yourself for hours in pornography might drown feelings of loneliness and low self-esteem. In order to overcome any addiction permanently, these deeper emotional needs must be identified and, if possible, resolved. It's important to remember that negative emotions are a part of life. We will all experience loneliness, boredom, frustration and a whole host of other difficult emotions at some stage in our lives. The key to permanent addiction recovery is to develop healthy strategies to manage these emotions rather than turning to a toxic behaviour that frequently creates the very emotions that the person is striving to avoid.

In this section we will explore some of the most common underlying issues that affect people with sex and porn addiction. I must highlight that this can be long term work. Some people find they need extensive personal therapy for this part of the recovery process, therefore what follows is simply an overview and additional resources will be required. This is especially true in the case of working with both trauma and attachment-induced addictions. We will go back to Craig to elucidate each element.

Exploring childhood issues

All of us carry baggage from our childhood and some is heavier than others. Our early childhood experiences influence how we feel about ourselves, how we relate to others, and how we interact with our world. It is likely that everyone with sex addiction, and many with pure porn addiction, will have picked up unhelpful messages about how to healthily regulate their emotions and meet their deepest needs. And people with an attachment-induced addiction may find their adult relationships are continually impacted by the messages they learnt in childhood about how to love and be loved. Those with a trauma-induced addiction who experienced abuse as a child are likely to have the deepest and most painful scars.

Some people come for addiction treatment already aware of the impact of their childhood, while others may describe their childhood as 'happy' and 'normal' until further exploration reveals hidden wounds. Some of the previous exercises in this book may have highlighted difficulties in childhood or problems that may have originated there. For example, if the assessment questionnaires in Chapter 2 have been completed, then you may already know if the addiction is opportunity-, trauma- or attachment-induced. In addition the core beliefs inventory in Chapter 10 may have highlighted areas of low self-esteem that had their roots in early childhood. There are a number of different strategies for exploring childhood. Some therapists use straightforward talk therapy, others prefer to use a history taking tool and some will take a developmental trauma inventory. In our work, we tend to favour a lifeline exercise which helps clients to notice, not just the negative times in their life, but also the positive ones, which often gives further insight into why particular acting out behaviours became the drug of choice. Whatever tool is used, it's better used within a therapeutic environment. Exploring childhood is a bit like farming a disused war field and you can never be sure when an unexploded landmine might be found, or worse still, detonated. Hence it's wise to work with an experienced therapist, trained in both addiction and childhood wounds, to avoid, or at least minimise, any possible explosions.

In therapy, Craig identified that whilst his childhood was mostly good, he had struggled when his parents separated when he was 14. His father left to be with someone else, explaining that he hadn't been happy in the relationship for years. Whilst both his parents tried to do their best for him, it was obvious that his mother was heartbroken and he felt torn between sympathy for his father and rage towards him. Money was tight because of the divorce and Craig realised that his resolution to study hard for a successful career and find the perfect partner came from a determination not to end up like his parents.

Managing negative emotions

In addition to exploring key childhood events, it's important to look at other significant emotions and how these were managed within the family of origin. Asking how key emotions such as anger, sadness and fear were expressed in the family can give important clues, as can asking what happened if you showed that you were angry, sad or fearful? We learn equally from what we see and do, and from what we know we're not meant to see and do.

For many people with addiction, individual, or sometimes group, therapy may provide the first safe opportunity for negative emotions to be expressed, emotions that may have been suppressed or repressed for a lifetime. Furthermore there is space to consider how these emotions can be accepted and integrated into self-identity and shared with others in a positive way.

Craig recognised that anger was an emotion that was almost never shown in his family. His parents never argued and never showed a negative emotion towards each other, even during the early days of their separation. As an only child, he also became aware of how often he felt lonely and how his commitment to school work had isolated him from others. He joined one of our recovery groups and for the first time felt able to share his anger at both of his parents, without being judged. He also enjoyed the camaraderie of being with others with whom he shared both good times and bad times alike.

Decision making, boundaries and self-control

As discussed in Chapter 3, many people with addiction come from backgrounds where there was either a rigid system of control or none at all. When children are not taught how to control themselves, they often grow up finding it difficult to make decisions that are based on an accurate assessment of their needs while considering the consequences. This then results in problems maintaining personal and relational boundaries.

During therapy, Craig was able to see how he learned to suppress both his emotions and his needs, often sublimating them to the greater needs of his parents. He recognised that whilst he found self-control easy when it came to work, he had never really learned how to have fun in a healthy way. He also realised that he had no concept of how to make decisions about, or within, a relationship. It was important for Craig not to feel that he was blaming his parents, as he felt they had brought him up as best they could, under very difficult circumstances. But having seen how the messages from his childhood had contributed to his porn addiction, he could now re-write them and choose a future that fitted with what he wanted for himself.

References

Voon, V., Mole, T.B., Banca, P., Porter, L., Morris, L., & Mitchell, S. *et al.* (2014) Neural correlates of sexual cue reactivity in individuals with and without compulsive sexual behaviours, *PloS ONE*, 9(7). Online. Available at http://journals.plos.org/plosone/article/asset?id=10.1371%2Fournal.pone.0102419.PDF (Accessed November 2017).

13 The C.H.O.I.C.E. recovery model
Identify positive sexuality

Being in recovery means giving up addiction, not giving up sex. Sex is great. It's fun, exciting, exhilarating, relaxing, romantic, intimate, erotic and esteem building. What's more, research suggests that it's good for our emotional and physical health as well as for our relationships (Whipple, 2003). Unfortunately, this is not true of *all* sex, as those who've suffered from sex or porn addiction and previous chapters of this book testify. But 'good' sex brings with it many benefits and a satisfying sex life is one of the most powerful relapse prevention strategies available.

When we talk about 'good' sex or 'positive sexuality,' we are not assuming this will be within a heterosexual monogamous relationship. People with sex or porn addiction come from every orientation and some choose open, non-monogamous sexual relationships, while others are single, or find themselves single. Whatever the relationship status, it's essential that the right to sexual expression is not ignored or minimised. Unlike any other substance addiction, the goal is not abstinence but healthy integration of positive sexuality. This means all expressions of sexuality should be considered including the choice of celibacy, casual sexual relationships, partnered sex, fetishes and masturbation. Each potential avenue needs to be explored in light of the impact it may have on the addiction, and whether the behaviour will perpetuate the cycle or help to break it.

In this chapter we will look at how positive sexuality can be achieved, whether someone is single or in a monogamous or open non-monogamous relationship. We will also explore how celibacy can be a positive sexual choice. You won't find any prescription for how to achieve positive sexuality as it differs for every individual and every relationship, and it is something that constantly evolves. But there is general information to guide your thinking and further reading suggestions are available in the resources section at the end of this book.

Defining 'positive' sexuality

Sexuality is the global term we use to describe our gender, our thoughts and our feelings about sex, be they positive or negative, our sexual orientation and desires, our sexual behaviours, including the choice of celibacy, and our sexual potential for reproduction and pleasure. We are all sexual in the same way as we are all emotional and we are all intellectual. Our emotional and intellectual capacity and expression may vary, but they nonetheless exist.

Being sexual is part of the nature of being human and, like emotion and thought, it is morally neutral. This is an important fact to acknowledge as it helps to break through shame, especially for those from sexually diverse communities who may have experienced shame in the past because of their sexual preferences. The state of 'being' is autonomous and affects no one. It is only when we are 'doing' that we begin to impact others. On the whole we don't make moral judgements about how others think and feel. Indeed, unless they choose to express it, we are unaware that there is anything to judge. It is only when emotion, thoughts and/or sexuality are expressed to the detriment of others that we should even consider making a judgement. Like emotion and intellect, our sexuality is one of the strategies we can call on for survival or we can use it for our individual pleasure or to communicate and build relationships with others. And in the same way as our emotions and thinking are not fully within our conscious control, neither is our sexuality. In short it is our choice how we express and manage our sexuality, but we may not always be able to choose how we experience it.

Learning to be comfortable with our sexuality is a crucial element of good mental and emotional health. Being comfortable does not necessarily mean we can express our sexuality any way our genitals desire, but means that we're able to acknowledge and respect our sexual feelings and choose to express them in ways that fit with our values and our chosen lifestyle.

So what is positive sexuality? In a nutshell it is any kind of sexual expression that is fulfilling emotionally, physically, psychologically and spiritually. I include 'spiritually' because for many people sex has a spiritual component, whether that's linked to a faith, or a way of articulating the profound feelings of intimacy and wellbeing that sex can evoke. In short, positive sexuality is:

- in line with personal values
- respectful of self and others
- pleasurable

- mutually fulfilling (when partnered)
- not shameful
- confidence and esteem building
- safe from risk of physical or psychological harm.

Sex and porn addiction can rob a person of seeing sex as a fulfilling part of their life, but when it's such an integral part of being human, re-discovering this experience is a fundamental component of long-term recovery. However, many people with sex addiction grew up with negative messages about sex and sexuality and have never experienced fulfilling sex, and some with porn addiction may never have experienced partner sex at all.

Identifying sexual messages

We learn about sex from a variety of sources. Initially this happens within the family home and later we learn from peers and partners. We also learn from our communities, our culture and from society, and increasingly we learn about sex through the media and online. There are often different sexual messages for men and for women, and whether you're straight or gay. Typically in western society, men are brought up to believe that sex is a powerful drive that they must learn to manage through will, and emotions have little to do with it. Conversely women may believe they are the bastions of sexual safety who must protect their bodies, hearts and souls from men's desires whilst denying any lust of their own. There are perhaps more mixed messages about sex today than there have ever been at any other time in history. While some strive for greater sexual liberation, others use statistics of sexual crime and abuse, and indeed sex addiction, as evidence that we should become more conservative. Defining our sexual beliefs and boundaries is challenging in a world that advocates freedom and diversity – but it is a task that each of us must embrace. Ideally, the tools for the job are provided in childhood, but unfortunately there are some family belief systems that do not support healthy sexual decision making.

Broadly speaking there are four sexual belief systems that families adopt and pass on to their children, each of which can have a negative impact on healthy sexual development. The most common ones are: 'sex is bad,' 'sex is the answer to everything,' 'sex is complicated' and 'sex does not exist.' It's an unfortunate reality that many families struggle to talk openly about sex and therefore most of the messages we receive are through our parents' behaviours, rather than through what they have overtly said. Those negative messages can then be compounded through adolescent sexual experiences, or a lack of them, and when combined with negative core beliefs can leave some people struggling to believe that positive sexuality is possible.

For many people in recovery, establishing a positive sex life takes patience and time as they build relationships and go through different phases of life. However, the first step required is to set sexual boundaries that fit with personal values and individual lifestyle choice. Those boundaries can change over time.

Setting sexual boundaries

The biggest difference between sex addiction and most other addictions is that total abstinence is not the goal. However, many treatment approaches and some 12-Step groups recommend complete abstinence from any kind of sexual activity, alone or partnered, in the early stages of recovery. The reason given for this is that it may give the brain time to restore balance, but while there is little neuropsychological evidence to support this, there is ample clinical experience that many people benefit. A period of abstinence provides space to focus on the self and others in a non sexual way and allows previously anaesthetised emotions to come to the surface. Abstinence can also eliminate the anxiety that sex is an essential need and provide the opportunity to practise alternative self-soothing techniques. Another benefit of a period of abstinence is that it allows natural libido to be discovered. Many people with sex and porn addiction believe they have a high sex drive, as we explored in Chapter 1, but in the same way as fasting allows us to get in touch with our appetite and become comfortable with passing feelings of hunger, abstinence allows the opportunity to experience sex drive and become comfortable with it. An abstinence period of between 30 and 90 days is often recommended but ultimately it's up to the individual to decide which behaviours are essential for sobriety and a timescale that works for them. Remember that it is the function of sexual behaviour that defines it as addiction, not the behaviour itself, therefore as long as the behaviour is 'positive' and does not trigger compulsivity, then there is probably no reason to abstain. However, before that decision can be made it's essential to confirm what your sexual boundaries are.

The circle exercise

This exercise has been adapted from the 3 circle exercise used by Sex Addicts Anonymous. To complete it, you first need to get a sheet of

Identify positive sexuality 157

paper and list every kind of sexual activity you have ever been involved in, alone and with other people. That might include masturbating with porn, masturbating without porn, having sex with a partner, engaging in cyber sex, telephone sex, viewing late night TV channels, voyeurism, visiting massage parlours, sex cinemas, sex workers, dogging sites, stranger sex, affairs, ChemSex, one night stands and so on and so on. Once this has been done, the challenge is to separate the list into the appropriate areas in Figure 13.1.

The top OK circle is where you write all the behaviours that fit with your values and that you are completely comfortable with. The bottom NOT OK circle is for the behaviours that are definitely outside of your value system. The overlap IFFY area is for those behaviours that you're still currently unsure about. You might be unsure because you don't know how you feel about a behaviour or whether it would cause a problem for a partner. You should also list here any behaviours that, although OK in themselves, might lead to the NOT OK circle. For example, someone whose addiction has been visiting sex workers may not have an addiction to internet pornography but they may put internet porn in their middle circle because they know they are much more likely to be tempted to visit sex worker sites when online. Most people are more comfortable doing this exercise alone where it may be easier to be completely honest and open about sexual behaviours. However, once completed, it's beneficial to discuss the OK and IFFY areas with a therapist, 12-Step sponsor, or trusted friend, who will challenge you if necessary. And eventually, a final decision needs to be

Figure 13.1 Circle exercise

made about where to put the IFFY behaviours. In early recovery, there should be nothing left in IFFY, especially if relapse is likely to be catastrophic to yourself or another. The circle exercise is one that can be reviewed at a later date when sobriety has been established, so at that point something that was previously IFFY may be moved to OK when you are confident it won't lead to relapse. But, in the early days of recovery, it is wiser to err on the side of caution.

Once this circle exercise has been completed and a decision has been made about what is OK and what is not OK, the next step, if it's not already been taken due to the crisis of discovery, is to stop. Some people just stop on their own, without telling anyone. Others become part of a recovery community, whether that's one of our recovery courses, a 12-Step group or an online community – all of which we will discuss more in Chapter 14. But however you stop, remember that it's equally important to start something else – to ensure you're getting on with building your new lifestyle and striving towards your vision as we explored in Chapter 11. Next we'll look at some of the particular challenges that some people face when trying to establish their new sexual lifestyle.

Sex when you are single

Struggling with sex addiction when you're single can present particular challenges when it comes to developing positive sexuality. Unlike the partnered addict who may just be stopping extra-relational sex, most single addicts will have to completely give up the sexual lifestyle they've previously experienced. For most, a period of celibacy and abstinence from masturbation can be useful to allow old neural pathways to begin to fade; however, if masturbation was never compulsive or a contributory factor, this may not be required.

Like someone who's in a relationship, it's essential to define positive sexuality and to ensure that desired behaviours are in line with personal values. Since sexual activity is almost inevitably going to be limited, if not absent for a while, alternative ways of achieving physical satisfaction should be explored. For some that might include taking up a new physical activity such as sport or exercise, or a body-awareness practice such as yoga or Qigong. For those who have given up masturbation, a new mindful approach that precludes fantasy needs to be established before restarting, to ensure the cycle is not re-triggered – more on this later in this chapter.

Understandably, many single addicts are keen to find a new relationship, but dating can offer additional dilemmas to someone who is in early recovery. Confidence needs to be gained that any motivation for being sexual does not come from the compulsion and there may be some behaviours within a new relationship, such as watching porn together, that could be triggering and hence need to be avoided. This may be difficult to do without being open about the problem with a new partner. In my experience, most people with an addiction would prefer their new partner to know of their history. Not only does this allow a truer experience of intimacy but it also opens the door for additional support and encouragement. However, timing is important and unfortunately it must be accepted that there is a risk that some prospective partners will choose to walk away.

Monogamous couple sex

For addicts who are continuing in a monogamous couple relationship, their list of OK behaviours needs to be explored in consultation with their partner. If there are activities missing that a partner would enjoy it will be necessary to explain that this could be triggering for the addict and hence needs to be avoided – at least in early recovery.

The discovery of sex or porn addiction can be devastating to couple relationships and many partners do not want to have any sexual contact until recovery for both has been established. However, when the time is right, recovery from addiction can provide an opportunity for couples to fully explore their sexual relationship and consider how they would like it to improve and grow. It can also be helpful to discuss what role sex has played in the couple relationship in the past and how they want it to feature in the future, remembering that sex changes over the course of a relationship and as we age, and that sex will inevitably mean different things at different times. Couples who have previously had an open or non-monogamous relationship who are committing to monogamy for the first time will also need to consider the implications and challenges of doing this and how they will be faced. There's much more on building a partnered sexual relationship in Sex Addiction – A Guide for Couples (publication date tbc).

Open non-monogamy

Some people with sex addiction are in open non-monogamous relationships. Open non-monogamy only works where there are clear boundaries that have been agreed between all involved. Most commonly this will be agreements around the amount of non-sexual involvement allowed and the types of sexual behaviours. For example, some swingers agree that they will be sexual with other people but preserve intercourse for their own relationship. When those boundaries are broken then there is a breach of trust and potential for all the accompanying difficulties that happen in any other intimate relationship.

When one partner within a non-monogamous relationship discloses sex addiction, the boundaries need to be redrawn by both. It is likely that the addicted partner will need to put firm restrictions on their own behaviour because they have broken the agreed boundaries. This will have an impact on everyone else within the relationship and hence agreeing new terms of engagement will be a larger task than for those in monogamous relationships. Often a primary partner's reaction is to see the addiction as proof that non-monogamy does not work for them and they may want to switch to monogamy. When this happens, both must seriously consider if this is viable for them as individuals and explore what will be lost, as well as what will be gained, if they become monogamous. For couples who have been openly non-monogamous for a long time, especially those on the gay or kink scene, the switch to monogamy may also have significant social implications.

Celibacy

Most people will not see celibacy as a sexual choice, but for many people recovering from addiction, especially those who are single, celibacy is an option to be seriously considered – at least for a while. Celibacy is a personal commitment to avoid any sexual relationship and traditionally was sometimes linked to a life-time religious vow. Nowadays, many people choose celibacy, or abstinence, as an alternative to casual sex or non-relational sex, and put fulfilment of their sexual desires on hold until they're in a committed relationship.

It would be nice to say that the key advantage of celibacy is that it is unambiguous, and while it is with regard to no partner sex, views on masturbation may differ. Some believe that celibacy should not include any kind of self-stimulation whereas others believe that releasing the occasional urge is OK. Ultimately each person must decide for themselves. The key to celibacy is that partner sex is taken out of the frame. If there is occasional masturbation, it is about scratching a biological itch to eliminate the urge rather than wanting sex per se, so that celibacy can be enjoyed again. The advantage of celibacy for someone recovering from sex addiction is that it allows time and energy to be fully focused on other areas of life. Having made the decision that sex is not on the agenda, there is space to grow and develop in other areas. Most find the discomfort of sexual desire gradually declines and relationships, new and old, take on a different quality when sex is not a goal. Like monogamy, and non-monogamy, celibacy has its challenges, but for some it's the simplest option.

Overcoming sexual challenges

Most people in recovery will face sexual challenges and this is especially true for those who may never have experienced 'sober' sex, or have forgotten what it is. For some the challenges will be an immediate and ongoing problem, especially in early recovery, while for others it may be something that occurs just occasionally. The challenges listed below are often difficult to discuss and manage in a couple situation without creating potential alarm and anxiety for partners, and hence it's usually better for these to be dealt with individually. If issues are particularly entrenched or persistent, referral to a psychosexual therapist would be advised.

Dealing with fantasies

Whether you call it fantasies or memories, the problem is the same, as visual images of what's been seen or experienced during acting out can become imprinted on the brain. These images can then arise uninvited during sexual activity, whether that's with a partner or alone. Blocking these images out takes time and perseverance. The most successful technique is to develop a habit of mindfulness during sex. This means staying fully present in the room with all the senses. Focusing on sight, smell, hearing, taste and especially physical sensation. This can be harder to achieve during masturbation when there is less sensory input and for this reason many addicts who are in a relationship choose not to masturbate. For those who are single, it's often best to set a period of abstinence during early recovery and only introduce masturbation when mindfulness skills have been developed and visual images can be controlled. More on this later in this chapter.

Diverting sexual frustration

Although sex and porn addiction are primarily used as a way of anaesthetising against negative emotions there's no denying the fact that for many they also provide sexual release. In the early stages of recovery some addicts experience a reduction in their sex drive. In part this may be due to feelings of shame and the stress of recovery, but it may also be due to the absence of their preferred stimuli. Many others struggle with unmet sexual needs. In order to manage the cravings for sexual satiation it first needs to be established that the need is truly sexual, rather than emotional. As discussed previously, when sexual release has been a bi-product of negative emotions it becomes a conditional response and hence difficult feelings trigger arousal. Therefore, when arousal is felt the first question is whether or not another unmet need is being stimulated. For example, if strong feelings of arousal happen after a stressful day at work, could the deeper need be for expressing frustration or having a friend to share the burden with? If sexual frustration is a significant issue then physical diversion such as exercise is generally an effective solution, but if feelings do not subside then this may be nature's way of telling you that you need physical release. If you don't have the option of partnered sex and you've chosen not to masturbate, then at some stage you're likely to have an orgasm in your sleep, or a wet-dream as it's often referred to for men. But if masturbation is in your OK circle and it's definitely triggered by libido, then mindful masturbation is an option.

Resolving sexual dysfunctions

Sexual dysfunctions are common in people with sex and porn addiction. Whilst they are most often a consequence of an artificially elevated arousal threshold, they are sometimes also a cause and unless resolved, will almost certainly perpetuate the addiction cycle. The most common dysfunctions are arousal and orgasmic disorders, such as delayed ejaculation and difficulty experiencing orgasm, problems with getting or maintaining an erection and low sexual desire. Unless addressed, relapsing to sexual acting out or porn will continue in order to re-establish sexual functioning. Common sexual dysfunctions include:

- *Low sexual desire* – This is common for many people in early recovery from sex or porn addiction and it often takes them by surprise. Some people with an addiction may have split off their sexuality to such an extent that couple sex was almost non-existent. Others feel so much shame about their behaviours that they can't bear to be intimate with a loved one. Some develop what's known as the Madonna/whore syndrome where women are split into either good girls who don't or bad girls who do. When this thinking is ingrained it can be difficult to feel desire for a partner who is seen as too special for sex while arousal is still present for others. Sometimes this situation resolves on its own as the couple relationships improve, whilst others find it beneficial to work with a therapist trained in psychosexual therapy.

- *Orgasmic disorders* – Delayed ejaculation for men and problems experiencing orgasm for women are commonplace for people who have become heavy porn users and, regrettably, this can lead either to relapsing with porn or fantasising about porn images in order to reach orgasm. Whilst most would agree that using fantasy is not as bad as actual acting out and that it will trigger climax, in the long run it will also maintain the requirement for high levels of stimulation and prolong the problem. Mindful masturbation, as detailed at the end of this chapter and/or psychosexual therapy can help to resolve this long-term.
- *Erectile difficulties* – As explored in Chapter 1, erectile dysfunctions or PIED (porn induced erectile dysfunction) is commonplace amongst heavy internet porn users. A period of abstinence may be all that's required to resolve the problem, but the problem can be further compounded within relationships when performance anxiety also kicks in. It's an unfortunate fact that the more you worry about getting an erection, the less likely you are to achieve one. If time doesn't resolve the issue, mindful masturbation can be used to develop erectile confidence and the skills transferred into couple sexual activity.

Mindful masturbation

Many people in the early stages of recovery struggle to enjoy any kind of self-touching without fantasy or concurrent drug use. Indeed, some people who have been brought up with internet porn, or frequent ChemSex users may doubt that it's even possible to get aroused, experience orgasm, or enjoy sex without fantasy or chems. Learning mindful masturbation has a number of benefits. First it begins to reprogramme the neural pathways to respond to touch. Second it provides essential practice in mindful sexuality that can be useful in partnered sex and finally, and perhaps most importantly, it proves that the body is capable of responding just through touch and provides a positive way of releasing sexual tension.

It's difficult to write out exactly how to masturbate mindfully, so what follows is an overview of the principles. For many, this is enough, but if you need further guidance then a few appointments with a psychosexual therapist who can tailor homework exercises for you will ensure you've mastered what you need to know. The metaphor I use when working with clients is this. Imagine you're sitting down to eat your absolute favourite, delicious, mouth-watering meal - would you put the television on while you eat or close your eyes and fantasise about eating something else? No of course not, you would almost rid yourself of all distractions and eat whilst relishing every taste and texture. In short, you would eat it mindfully and that is how you have to start enjoying masturbation, and of course, partnered sex.

If you want to learn mindful masturbation, then start practicing the skills during meals. Pay full attention to every mouthful, every smell, taste, texture. Be fully present. Once you're able to achieve that, then you can begin to pay attention to your body mindfully. Next time you take a shower or have a bath, focus on the sensation of the water. Feel the temperature, the sensations on your skin and when you're clean, dry yourself mindfully taking time to 'feel' every inch of your skin. As you're drying your genitals, take a little extra time to notice the different sensations and sensitivities. The objective isn't to get aroused, but simply to focus and build the neural connections around touch.

When you're ready, move on to more arousing genital touch, really taking your time to experiment with different strokes and pressures. At first you may find that you don't get aroused and that's fine. It can take a few weeks of practice before your body begins to respond. When you do notice that you're getting an erection, stop for a while and let the feeling subside, then begin again. Don't rush the process. Remember it took your body many, many months, perhaps years of heavy porn use to get to the place it is now, it may take quite a few 'mindful' experiences before it gets used to responding simply to your touch. If you continue to struggle after some weeks of practicing these exercises, or if you find mindful masturbation difficult to translate into a partner setting, then you might find it beneficial to book some sessions with a sex therapist who can tailor exercises for your individual needs.

Identifying positive sexuality is essential to secure long-term recovery, and indeed, being able to express our sexuality in an affirming way is a basic human right. Remember you can choose how you want your sex life to be and how important a part it will play in your life and in your relationship. It will take time for old habits to change, psychologically and physically, but I'm pleased to say that there are many hundreds of men and women out there in recovery who enjoy sex more now than they ever did during their addiction.

References

Hall, P. (date tbc) *Sex Addiction: A Guide for Couples*, Routledge, London.
Whipple, R. (2003) *White Paper: The Health Benefits of Sexual Expression*, Planned Parenthood Federation of America in Cooperation with the Society for the Scientific Study of Sexuality.

14 The C.H.O.I.C.E. recovery model
Connect with others

'The opposite of addiction is not sobriety, the opposite of addiction is connection.' This was the closing line of Johann Hari's thought provoking TED talk in 2014 where he eloquently explained the now infamous rat park experiment and why addicts, those who care about them, and policy makers need to learn from its findings. The rat park experiment was undertaken by Bruce Alexander back in the 70s in an attempt to challenge existing research that had been done. Earlier experiments had shown that when you put a rat in a cage with two bottles, one containing pure water and the other water laced with either cocaine or heroin, the rat favours the latter. And almost 100 percent will use the drug-filled bottle to the point of overdose and death. This experiment was used for many years to further the argument that exposure to drugs will inevitably lead to addiction. Alexander's hypothesis was that perhaps it was the cage that was the problem, rather than the drug. To test this he created Rat Park. Rat park was a large cage with a community of rats who had toys to play with, lots of tasty food, and the two bottles, one pure water, the other laced with drugs. In Rat Park almost all of the rats preferred the pure water and of those who did occasionally use the drug bottle, 0 percent used it compulsively. The conclusion drawn was that that if you change the environment and provide community, addiction does not occur.

Of course the problem is that humans are not rats and whilst creating rat heaven may be relatively easy, human heaven is much harder to achieve. Rat Park also failed to include rats who'd experienced childhood trauma or rats who'd received questionable parenting or rats who struggled with low self esteem, but nonetheless, it did demonstrate that addiction is about much, much more than biology and when community is available, drugs lose their appeal. And this is true whether your drug of choice is chemical or sexual. In this chapter we will explore the different ways in which we can connect with others and why this is so important for long-term recovery from sex and porn addiction recovery.

Why connect?

As a species, humans need each other to survive and thrive. Countless research papers have been written about the importance of human attachment for good mental health. Indeed, the core principle of the 12-Steps is connecting with others and is undoubtedly the reason for its success. Back in Chapter 3 we explored how early attachment ruptures can lead to addiction and those with an attachment-induced addiction will need to prioritise building relationships as part of their recovery. But all of us need others who we trust to love and care for us, as well as people to give our love to. It is only within the presence of others that we can gain a true and accurate sense of ourselves. Our relationships are like mirrors within which we have the chance to see in ourselves what others see. Some of that may be uncomfortable, but it can be an encouragement to change, and hopefully much of it will be positive which can strengthen self-esteem, reduce shame and reinforce our own lovability. It is only within relationships that we can experience a sense of sameness and belonging; knowing that others are just like us and that we are 'normal.' Conversely it is within relationships that we can learn about our uniqueness, the ways that we differ, our strengths and our weaknesses. We can learn alternative views of seeing and being in the world that can both challenge us and encourage us to grow.

The way we relate to others is often developed in childhood and the pattern of relating that we develop is often referred to as an attachment style. These styles of relating continue into adulthood and are often consciously and unconsciously reinforced. Once we're aware of our attachment style we then have the opportunity to explore whether it is helpful or unhelpful in our lives and we can choose to change it. Below is a list of common attachment styles – have a look and see, which best describes you.

- *The Anxious Attacher* – someone who is an anxious attacher frequently feels insecure in relationships. They may be jealous and needy of attention and require regular reassurance that they're liked, loved and valued. They may be particularly sensitive to perceived criticism and either consciously, or unconsciously spend a lot of time seeking validation. Anxious attachers are often chameleons,

constantly adapting themselves in order to fit in and feel a sense of belonging.
- *The Avoidant Attacher* – people with an avoidant attachment style would probably describe themselves as someone who likes their own space. Although they enjoy the company of others, they can easily feel suffocated and tend to withdraw to meet their own needs. They find it difficult to trust other people and avoid commitment. Avoidant attachers usually pride themselves on their independence and can often end relationships with relative ease.
- *The Ambivalent Attacher* – ambivalent attachers, sometimes known as disorganised attachers, find themselves flitting between anxious and avoidant. They crave intimacy and affection but are also fearful of it and consequently may be somewhat erratic in their behaviour within relationships. Ambivalent attachers can swing between being needy one minute to being rejecting and fiercely independent the next. They can also struggle with commitment because as soon as they feel they can rely on somebody, they withdraw to avoid rejection.
- *Secure attacher* – secure attachment is what we all want to have. When someone has a secure attachment they are able to commit themselves to relationships, knowing that some experiences may be positive, but sometimes they may get hurt. But when they are hurt, they're able to self-soothe in healthy ways and either resolve the issues in the relationship or move on.

When it comes to sex and porn addiction, an anxious attacher is likely to be someone who needs multiple relationships in order to achieve the attention and validation they desire. They will be particularly attracted to adult hook up sites and sex parties where they can receive lots of positive affirmation. The avoidant attacher may feel safer with pornography and paid-for sex where there is little or no emotion or affection and the ambivalent attachers may use casual sex to gain what is perceived as safe intimacy without commitment; or they may seek additional partners or a secret world of porn to ward off fears of rejection or suffocation within their primary relationship.

Attachment styles are based on two factors, how we perceive others and how we perceive ourselves. When we are comfortable with others, and ourselves, we are likely to develop a secure attachment that results in healthy, fulfilling relationships. Many addicts have either an anxious attachment style that constantly seeks intimacy whilst being fearful of hurt; or an avoidant attachment style that is mistrustful of others and strongly independent; or an ambivalent attachment style which fears intimacy but also fears being alone. Having identified which style is favoured work can start on developing a secure attachment style that is comfortable both with intimacy and with independence and, critically, is able to confidently self-soothe when relationships hurt.

An unhealthy attachment style often results in a number of 'relational needs' becoming neglected and it is often these needs that are sought out in acting out behaviours. For some, a couple relationship may be too risky a place to ask for those needs to be met since being rejected would be too painful. For others, a sense of safe independence can only be felt if some needs are kept outside of a partnered relationship. Once these needs have been identified, work can begin to explore how these relational needs may be met by connecting with others.

Identifying relational needs

The term 'relational needs' came from the school of integrative psychotherapy where eight foundational needs were established as the essential building blocks for good mental health and relationship functioning (Erskine et al., 1999). Those needs are listed below.

1. *Security* – our need to feel safe in our relationships with others, knowing that we're free from threats of shame, attack, abandonment and engulfment.
2. *Validation* – knowing our feelings and identity are unconditionally accepted by another, including having our relational needs accepted and affirmed.
3. *Acceptance* by a stable, dependable and protective other person – this is about our need to have someone in our lives who we can trust and who we know is looking out for us.
4. *Confirmation of personal experience* – this defines our need to have someone who is similar to us. Someone who has been through similar experiences.
5. *Self-definition* – our need to feel separate, autonomous and unique.
6. *The need to have an impact on other people* – in order for us to feel satisfied in our relationships, we need to know that what we do and who we are can influence another in a positive way.
7. *The need to have another initiate* – to know that someone else will reach out to us and want to make contact, rather than always being the person who makes the first move.

8 *The need to give love* – we all have an inbuilt need to love and to be able to show our love for another.

The fewer the relational needs that are met, the more likely we are to feel alone and isolated. This is true even for people who would say they are very sociable and have many friends. I know it's a cliché, but it's true that quality counts more than quantity. Having lots of 'mates' that rarely call you and only seem to enjoy your company when you're cracking a joke, but don't have any idea of the struggles you face, is not enough. Similarly having a partner who loves you and depends on you wholly, but feels threatened any time you want to do something alone and can't bear for you not to be 'the strong one' leaves many needs unmet.

Regrettably our culture tells us that a couple relationship should be all we need. Phrases like 'you're all I need' and 'you complete me' are considered romantic, but they're both unreasonable and unrealistic. A single person will never be enough to meet all our relational needs, and certainly not all of the time, and hence we need a number of close relationships. We will now go on to look at the different kinds of relationships where we can connect and meet our relational needs, starting with couple relationships – but please note, this list is not in order of importance!

Couple relationships

When recovering from sex addiction, having a fulfilling and stable couple relationship can be both a support and an incentive. For many people, a happy couple relationship is one of the most important things in their lives, a place where they can love and be loved, where they can find peace, comfort and support as well as stimulation and pleasure, a place that provides a refuge from the struggles of life. Therefore it's perhaps not surprising that the quality of the couple relationship is a key influencer of successful lifelong recovery. An unhappy or unfulfilled couple relationship can put a huge strain on every area of life, but regrettably, as we explored in Chapter 5, the discovery of sex and porn addiction can inevitably push relationships to breaking point. Improving couple relationships needs to be a key focus in recovery, but as partners need time to come to terms with what's happened and make their decision about the future of the relationship, there may be many months before the relationship can be repaired, let alone improved. You'll find a lot more help on improving couple relationships in Sex Addiction – A Guide for Couples (tbc) and also further reading at the end of this book. But in the meantime, there are other relationships that can be worked on now.

Friends

A friend in need is a friend indeed, or so the saying goes, and recovery is a time when friends can play an especially important role. Many people with an attachment-induced addiction would say they've never really had any close friends and all tend to find that their compulsive behaviours have meant that they've kept people at arm's length. The shame of sex addiction often leaves people unable to fully relax in others' company and inevitably this can affect the bond of friendship. Friendships fulfil many different functions, but all provide an opportunity to connect with others and broaden our lives.

Different types of friendships can be extremely valuable in recovery. Having a best friend to confide in provides a space to share struggles and victories and receive encouragement, as well as a place where you can escape from your own problems for a while and listen to theirs. Other friends may know nothing about the addiction, but they are equally valuable as a place for relaxation and fun that can provide well earned respite in the early stages of recovery as well as creating a healthier lifestyle.

An exercise that clients often find helpful is to draw concentric circles (as in Figure 14.1), marking themselves in the centre and then writing down the names of friends in the extending circles, based on how close or distant they feel. This can then be used as a template to consider the friendships that you would like to develop and draw closer.

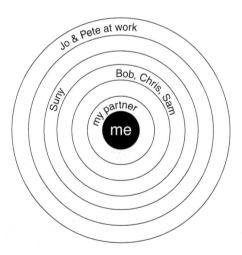

Figure 14.1 Concentric circle exercise

Family

They say you can choose your friends, but not your family and that is of course very true, but you can choose how close you want to be to them. That may not be possible if members of your family have made a decision to exclude you, but assuming that's not the case, then you have a significant role to play in how much time you spend with family members and the quality of that time.

Family means different things to different people and at different stages of life. Family may mean parents and siblings or it may mean grown up children and grandchildren; or it may include aunts, uncles, cousins and grandparents too. It may also include step and foster family members. Whatever the shape and style of your family, you will inevitably feel closer to some than others. It's been said that addiction isn't a spectator sport; eventually the whole family gets to play. And that is true whether your family knows about the addiction or not. The secrecy of addiction separates families, slowly and steadily, and disclosure can bring some family members much closer but might drive others apart. One of the saddest things I have heard in therapy is how the escalation of addiction has created more and more invisible barriers between loved ones, especially between a parent and children. As the shame increases, the sense of hypocrisy grows and parents with addiction often find themselves withdrawing more and more from intimate connection with their children. Recovery provides the opportunity to deepen relationships again and be fully present, rather than preoccupied with future or past acting out. And it provides a chance to nurture relationships with people who have known you long before you were an addict, and people who you share your everyday life with. As family becomes an increasingly stable base, addiction is easier to fight. It may take time, and perhaps some personal sacrifice, but it's time well worth spending.

Therapeutic recovery groups

It's hard to put into words the profound impact that recovery groups have on people's lives and it's often not until you've experienced it personally that you can truly understand. The Hall Recovery Course is the bedrock of the work we do at the Laurel Centre and is undoubtedly the most rewarding work we do, both for us as therapists and for our clients. For those with an attachment-induced addiction I would go so far as to say that group work is essential for recovery. Trying to recover from attachment wounds without a group is like trying to learn to swim from a book. You can learn the theory through individual therapy, but at some stage you have to get in the water. I have worked with clients who have had years of individual therapy, moving in and out of recovery with greater or lesser success, who then go on one of our programmes and change almost overnight. One client said '*I never imagined that I could learn more about myself in the last 7 days than I have in the last 30 years.*' A group recovery course can be life changing, not because of what you learn (though that is part of it), but because of the way you learn it and who you learn it with. I'm going to let the following quotes from previous course attendees speak for themselves:-

> 'The group recovery course was a life affirming, life changing experience that started with six disparate, scared, lonely blokes who all underwent a journey of self discovery and ended with six comrades so much better equipped to deal with the challenges of life and addiction.'

> 'I started the course full of trepidation and feeling alone with my problem. I left the course full of hope and with a network of support from my fellow recovering addicts. Thank you for giving my life meaning again.'

> 'A powerful experience. It is natural to feel apprehension about working in a group. Having been through the experience I can testify that it is the most powerful part of the programme. Don't underestimate the power of a collective!'

> 'I thoroughly enjoyed the course, most of all the bond that I built up with the guys. I found the advice and exercises very, very useful and I hope to have made some friends that will last for many years.'

> 'The exercises and work done in groups is not the only benefit. I have made many good friends and a network of support even after the group course has finished.'

> 'Having tried one-to-one therapy on a number of occasions without long term success I found out about Paula's group therapy and decided to set aside my initial reservations about discussing my problem with others. This undoubtedly proved to be one of the best decisions of my life and the cohesiveness of our group has provided invaluable support to me in my recovery, which as I

write, is in its sixteenth month. Group therapy allows you to contribute to, and benefit from, a valuable long term support network of people who truly understand the nature of sex and porn addiction.'

In my experience, the people who want to do group work the least are the ones who need it most. If your reaction is 'I'm scared of being judged' or 'I won't fit in' or 'It's just not me' – then you're probably an anxious, avoidant or ambivalent attacher – and that is precisely why you need to jump in the water and learn to swim!

12-Step fellowships

We began to explore the 12-Steps in Chapter 8, where I shared my concern about mentioning them within the context of a chapter on spirituality. Whilst there is a spiritual dimension to the 12-Step fellowships, the real power comes from the opportunity they provide to connect with others. Attending a 12-Step meeting should not be seen as an alternative to individual therapy or attending a therapeutic recovery group, but as an essential addition (assuming there are fellowships in your geographic region). A 12-Step programme can be particularly effective at establishing sobriety, while some kind of therapy is usually required to cement recovery. One of the great strengths of the group element within a 12-Step fellowship is the opportunity to meet people who are further along their recovery journey, people who have been sober for many months or years. In addition to peer support at meetings, the 12-Step groups also provide individual guidance through the 12-Step programme through volunteer sponsors who have already completed the steps themselves.

As said in Chapter 8, the steps themselves are often seen as confusing and overly spiritual. In part this is because they were written many years ago from a spiritual perspective and whilst the meaning has evolved, some of the language hasn't. Below is a list of the 12-Steps used by SAA, along with a simplified meaning, which hopefully expresses the principle of each step in plain English.

There are currently three different groups that provide help for sex and porn addiction. SAA (Sex Addicts Anonymous), SLAA (Sex & Love Addicts Anonymous) and SA (Sexaholics Anonymous). Each group works under slightly different parameters with SA considered the most conservative with their stipulation that only heterosexual marital sex is permissible. Probably due to this rigidity, SAA and SLAA are

Table 14.1 SAA 12-Step programme

	Traditional	*Simplified*
Step 1	We admitted we were powerless over addictive sexual behavior – that our lives had become unmanageable	I've got a problem
Step 2	Came to believe that a Power greater than ourselves could restore us to sanity	I need help and help is out there
Step 3	Made a decision to turn our will and our lives over to the care of God as we understood God	I will ask for help
Step 4	Made a searching and fearless moral inventory of ourselves	I'll work out what's wrong with me
Step 5	Admitted to God, to ourselves, and to another human being the exact nature of our wrongs	I'll share what's wrong with me with someone
Step 6	Were entirely ready to have God remove all these defects of character	I'm willing to change
Step 7	Humbly asked God to remove our shortcomings	I'll accept help to change
Step 8	Made a list of all persons we had harmed and became willing to make amends to them all	I'll work out who I've hurt and do something about it
Step 9	Made direct amends to such people wherever possible, except when to do so would injure them or others	I will repair relationships when I can
Step 10	Continued to take personal inventory and when we were wrong promptly admitted it	I accept that I will make mistakes but I will resolve them when I do
Step 11	Sought through prayer and meditation to improve our conscious contact with God as we understood God, praying only for knowledge of God's will for us and the power to carry that out	I will stay connected to others and be accountable
Step 12	Having had a spiritual awakening as the result of these steps, we tried to carry this message to other sex addicts and to practice these principles in our lives	I will help others

generally more popular groups and more appropriate for most people. Whilst each group is different, so also is each fellowship within the group. Some fellowships are thriving, whilst others struggle, but all are completely confidential and there is no compulsory fee to attend. There can be great knowledge, experience and wisdom within the members of the fellowships, as well as within the steps themselves, which is hard to rival in any other context. And like the therapeutic recovery groups, they provide a safe space to break through isolation and shame and experience both receiving and giving, validation and support.

The irony of addictive behaviours is that they are so often used to ease the pain of loneliness and isolation, but they actually create more. The secrecy and shame of being dependent on porn, betraying a loved one, or only being able to have sex when drunk or high on drugs, results in us avoiding intimacy rather than creating it and nurturing it. When we can connect with others and build relationships where our relational needs are being met, not only can we feel supported in recovery, but we begin to heal the wounds that cause and maintain the addiction. I'm sure there are many people who have stopped an addiction without connecting to others, but it's questionable whether they are truly living a recovered life or white-knuckling through abstinence.

References

Alexander, B.K. (2001) *Addiction: The View from Rat Park*, Simon Frazer University, Vancouver.

Erskine, R.G., Moursaund, J.P., & Trautmann, R.L. (1999) *Beyond Empathy: A therapy of contact in relationship*, Routledge, London.

Hall, P. (tbc), *Sex Addiction: A Guide for Couples*, Routledge, London.

15 The C.H.O.I.C.E. recovery model
Establish confident recovery

A client in recovery recently shared with me that he'd calculated how many hours each week he used to spend on his addiction and had decided that to establish his recovery, he needed to spend the 'same' amount of time on positive, healthy behaviours. This was a very wise insight, one that demonstrates an important fact – recovery is not about what you 'give up,' but what you 'take up.' In this chapter we will be focussing on what you need to take up to establish confident recovery, strategies that will help you to avoid slips and relapses and ensure you *enjoy* recovery, rather than endure it.

The types of activities that you might take up can be divided into two categories, daily disciplines and healthy pursuits and pastimes, in addition you'll need to work on managing emotions in a healthy way and recognise and overcome any blocks to recovery. We will look at each of these elements in depth, but first it's important to understand how and why relapse happens, and hence why working on these areas is essential for long-term, confident recovery.

Understanding relapse

Relapse is not an event, it's a process, explains Steven Melemis, author of 'I want to change my life,' and when this is understood, relapse can be avoided. In the early stages of recovery, this may be less true, while the brain is still dominated by dopamine and withdrawal may be at its worst. But as recovery is established, say six months in, one of the most common reasons people relapse is because they have not understood the process of relapse and taken adequate steps to stop it. Melemis explains the three stages of relapse as follows:-

- *Emotional relapse* – During this first stage, you're not tempted to act out and aren't even thinking about it. But life is beginning to

get on top of you. You may be going through a particularly stressful period through no fault of your own and emotions are getting difficult to manage. You'll probably have put a lot of your usual recovery and self-care routines on the shelf for a while, telling yourself you'll get back to these when you have more time.
- *Mental relapse* – Once you've been in emotional relapse for a while, you'll move into mental relapse. This is when you start thinking about your old acting out behaviours and triggers become more apparent. Some of the old cognitive distortions may come back, *'it's not that bad,'* *'I need/deserve this right now,'* or *'no-one would blame me.'* A common distortion during mental relapse is *'I've conquered my addiction now, I've proved I can do it, so now I'll be in control if I act out'* or *'I'll just act out once and see if it's as powerful as it used to be, I probably won't enjoy it after all this time.'* Chances are that you won't be telling anyone what's going on in your head and the longer that's the case, the greater the chance you'll move into physical relapse.
- *Physical relapse* – So this is the stage when you actually do act out. It may only be once, it may be gradual, at first ten minutes of porn here and there, checking a few online profiles, seeing if any old friends are still on Grindr, but sooner than you ever would have thought possible, you'll be back in full relapse.

When you understand how relapse happens and you learn to recognise the signs, then you can avoid it. We're all guilty of putting self-care to one side when we're busy or stressed. Exercise goes out of the window, we snack and live on fast food, we get less sleep, postpone social engagements with friends and the only relaxation time, if we're lucky, is an occasional mindless TV programme. We might know we're more irritable than usual and getting over reacting to minor things, but we tell ourselves *'when I'm through this, I'll get back to normal.'* Or if we're going through a stressful time because we're caring for others, we may feel guilty taking time for ourselves. But this kind of thinking is crazy, for everyone, because the more we care for ourselves, the more capacity we have to manage stress effectively and care for others. Furthermore, for people with addiction, the consequences of not looking after ourselves can be catastrophic.

If you're feeling stressed or going through an especially emotional time, or indeed if you know there is one coming up, now is the time to do *more* self-care, not less. Daily disciplines are a necessity, not an optional extra and continuing to keep life in balance with healthy pursuits and pastimes is what will keep your life wheel rolling through difficult times, rather than crashing into addiction. We'll look further at what those things might be in a moment, but first we'll explore the differences between a slip and a relapse and why it's so important to understand the difference.

Slip or relapse?

It's an unfortunate reality that many people with addiction will at times 'slip up' and a few will experience a full relapse. Distinguishing between the two is important as it's much easier to recover from a slip than a relapse and it prevents a momentary lapse of judgement or self-discipline getting worse. A slip has been explained as a Short Lapse In Progress – in other words, if someone addicted to pornography goes online for ten minutes after weeks without, this would be a slip. Similarly, if someone hasn't visited a sex worker in months but then makes an appointment but leaves before using their services, this would also be a slip. Although this is obviously not good for recovery, it would be a mistake to categorise it as a relapse since doing so can so easily invite the cognitive distortion *'I've already blown it, so I might as well go all the way.'* Having said that, when there are multiple, repeated slips, it's important not to distort reality by saying *'they're only slips.'* Whilst there may some truth in that, if you're slipping on a regular basis, you are on the precipice of a relapse.

Whether someone experiences a slip or a relapse, the most important thing is to manage the associated shame, recommit to recovery and get back on track again. Whilst no-one wants to experience slips or relapses, there are always lessons to be learned, whether that's the need to focus more on self-care, spend more time connecting with others, getting back to 12-Step meetings or individual therapy. Slips and relapses do not have to be an automatic consequence of addiction. Once you have made a choice to get into recovery, they can become a thing of the past. But if either do occur, embrace it as an opportunity to learn more about yourself and re-double your efforts on daily disciplines and throw yourself into even more healthy pursuits and pastimes – which we'll move on to look at now.

Daily disciplines

We all have daily disciplines and routines, many of which are linked to self-care, and they're such regular habits that it would feel odd not to do them. In the morning we brush our teeth, get washed, comb our hair, maybe check the news and the weather report, and of course, have that essential first cuppa. At night we lock the doors, turn the lights off, brush our teeth again and set the alarm. Some days are slightly different, if you're lucky you have a little more time and may enjoy a leisurely breakfast and read the news more thoroughly, before doing a bit of life maintenance such as laundry and tidying up. When you're in recovery you need to develop additional disciplines that soon become your regular routines – things that simply become 'what you always do.' Below we're going to look at what some of those things may be – they're in no order of importance, because they are ALL important.

Connect with others

We spent the whole of the last chapter talking about why connecting with others is so important and this needs to become a daily discipline. Ideally that is going to include a combination of friends, family and of course your primary relationship. But it's also important to connect with other people in recovery. In the early stages, daily connection is recommended, and once you're six months in, hopefully it will have become a habit. That might mean calling someone in a 12-Step fellowship or a fellow member of a recovery group, or someone who has agreed to be an accountability partner, such as a close friend, church member or therapist. It doesn't matter who it is, but connecting on a daily basis reminds you that you are in recovery and can provide invaluable support and motivation. A phone call is ideal, but if that's impractical, then a text or social media message is better than nothing. It makes it difficult to act out when you know you're going to speak to them again tomorrow!

Physical health

'Healthy body, healthy mind' is a well-known cliché that we increasingly accept as truth. When our body is strong we're more resilient to physical and emotional stress. We're more able to fight off viruses and infections, and we have more willpower to fight off triggers and temptations. Physical and mental agility allows us to remain vigilant to threat of every kind and, when recovering from addiction, that's vital. Our physical health can be optimised by paying *daily* attention to the following:

- *Sleep* – It's well known that sleep is essential for our physical health and wellbeing, and it's recommended that adults get 8 hours sleep per night. Many people with sex and porn addiction will

have lost their natural sleep routine, as the early hours are often a popular time for acting out. Developing a good sleeping habit will not only aid physical health but also provide the means for enough energy to pursue more productive pleasures.
- *Exercise* – When we exercise we automatically trigger our natural feel-good chemicals. Whether that's running, going to the gym, playing competitive sports or something more peaceful like Pilates or tai chi. Exercise can help relieve stress and reduce depression, both of which are common factors in addiction, and it can be a great way of filling time that had previously been taken up with acting out.
- *Diet* – In addition to maintaining a healthy diet of sufficient calorific intake and an appropriate balance of proteins, complex carbohydrates and fresh fruit and vegetables, supplements are also thought to aid recovery. As yet there is no clinical evidence to support the claims, but some believe that the addition of appropriate amino acids that serve as the building blocks for serotonin, dopamine and GABA can help in relapse prevention. Supplements may help restore deficiencies in these neurotransmitters and hence spur cravings and assist in finding alternative natural 'highs.' The main recommendations are 5HTP, L-Tyrosine, L-Tryptophan and L-Glutamine. If you would like further advice or information I would recommend seeing a reputable dietician.

Relaxation

Evidence suggests that regular daily relaxation, for a minimum of 20 minutes, relaxes our bodies for not only those 20 minutes but for the rest of the day. This is similar to what we know about exercise – regular exercise increases our metabolic rate, not just when we exercise, but permanently. To minimise stress, we need to consciously relax our mind and our body *every* day. Many people find mindfulness a useful way of doing this and utilise one of the mindfulness apps such as Headspace. For others it's meditation, whether with a religious focus or not and others use visualisation or simply give themselves time to sit and stare. It doesn't matter how you do it, as long as you do and you make it a regular part of your daily routine.

Journaling

Journaling is a discipline that many find invaluable in recovery. This involves taking some time at the end of each day to reflect on how the day has been, both high points and low, and to make note of the positive action they have taken that day. It's a great way of tracking progress on SMART goals (as discussed in Chapter 11) and ticking them off when complete. Many also use their journal as a place to make note of things people have said in meetings that they want to remember and insights gained in therapy sessions. Journaling can be a great tool for maintaining motivation as you can look back and see the progress you've made. It's tempting only to journal when times are tough, but by writing down the good times too, the journal becomes a resource for remembering that there probably many more good days than you think.

Gratitude

'Count your blessings' may be a well-worn platitude, as is 'develop an attitude of gratitude,' but they really do work. Many people in recovery use their journal as a resource to write a daily gratitude list. Daily gratitude helps to develop optimism because it forces you to be conscious of the positives in your life. If there are days when you're struggling to think of anything, catching up on the news is usually an effective way of jogging your memory!

Spiritual exercises

We talked a lot about spirituality in Chapter 8 and the many different forms that this can take. For someone in recovery, a spiritual exercise may be meditation, spending time appreciating nature, reading inspirational recovery literature or religious texts, or prayer.

Prayer is an important discipline for many in recovery, whether they have a religious belief or not. If you believe in God or a higher power, then you will be praying with a sense that someone is (hopefully) listening. But many atheists also say they pray, or at least that's the best definition they have for the conversations they have in their head. Prayer can be thought of as a way of expressing struggles to someone, or something, who won't judge or give advice. It can be helpful for self-reflection and if you're using a set prayer, such as those used in 12-Step or religious fellowships, it provides a way of reminding yourself of truths you want, or need, to hear. The most common prayer used in recovery is the Serenity prayer by Reinhold Niebuhr and whatever your spiritual persuasion, it's difficult not to recognise and value the wisdom of the words and have a desire to follow them.

The Serenity Prayer

> God, grant me the serenity to
> Accept the things I cannot change,
> the Courage to change the things I can,
> and the Wisdom to know the difference.
> Amen

Healthy pursuits and pastimes

Giving up an addiction will leave a hole in your life, both in terms of time and also in terms of reward, but there are an endless number of things you can do instead. Developing healthy pursuits and pastimes serves a number of functions. In addition to providing a distraction if triggered, they can also give a sense of purpose to life and an essential opportunity for fun and recreation, and an alternative way of getting a dopamine hit. Many activities can also provide an opportunity to experience 'flow,' and it's now widely understood that flow activities are a key contributor to recovery.

Understanding flow

Flow is used to describe the state of mind when we're totally absorbed by an activity, so absorbed that we're not distracted by anything else (Csikszentmihalyi, 2002). It's a state of mind, also known as being 'in the zone,' or 'in the groove,' where we are fully alert, yet relaxed, and we lose all concept of time. One of the attractions of addictions is that they are flow activities; we become completely absorbed by them and forget everything else. Long-term recovery means finding alternative ways to experience the positive emotions of flow; finding activities we can lose ourselves in and forget the everyday stresses and strains of life. A flow activity is characterised by finding just the right balance between ability and challenge. If something is too challenging, or too easy for us, we will become frustrated or bored. Hence finding activities where you can continue to feel challenged and continue to develop the necessary skills and abilities to meet that challenge, will be a flow activity. Almost anything can be a flow activity – it's not about what you do, but how you do it; how much you're willing to commit to becoming better at it.

Remember, recovery is not about what you give up, but what you take up. Below is a list of activities you might want to consider. Some may be old pursuits you used to enjoy or hobbies you always intended doing 'one day.' Some are things you may never have thought of before. Most can become flow activities and some have the added advantage of being social − so you can tick the 'connect to others' box at the same time!

- *Music* – listening to music, singing (whether that's karaoke, in a band or in a choir), playing a musical instrument or learning to play one; going to music concerts and shows.
- *Reading* – this might include self-help books and recovery literature, but also novels, poetry, autobiographies, learning about a particular topic or time in history. If reading's your thing, maybe join a book club as well to give you extra motivation.
- *Broadcasting* – including watching films, a drama series, comedy, quiz shows, natural history, educational programmes and documentaries. Also listening to radio shows, podcasts and audio books. There's an endless variety available now on almost any portable device.
- *Creativity* – that could be taking up art, pottery, photography, cooking, baking, sculpting, woodwork, knitting, writing, model-making, rug-making, DIY – the list is endless. Do something that will allow you to make something and give you a sense of achievement and pride.
- *Nature* – another potentially endless list. As well as visiting and enjoying nature, I'll also include here activities such as gardening, walking, cycling, fishing, horticulture, pot-holing, caving, mountain-climbing or biking. You can passively enjoy natural beauty, or be active within it.
- *Heritage and Culture* – visiting museums, art galleries, stately homes, theatre, opera, cinema, music and literary festivals. Consider also joining an amateur dramatic group or re-enactment group or learning acting or circus skills.
- *Sport and Fitness* – these could be team sports such as football, rugby, basketball, cricket or hockey, or something more solitary such as paragliding, swimming, yoga, Pilates, martial arts, athletics, running, kayaking, or paddle boarding, or something semi-social, such as skiing, scuba diving, shooting, archery, boxing, snooker, pool, dancing, darts, badminton, squash or tennis. Nearly all sports and fitness activities have clubs you can join to either compete or simply share the experience with others and maintain motivation.
- *Community work* – that could be joining a local volunteer group to help others within the community or contribute to an

environmental project, or volunteering at a local museum, or joining St John's Ambulance, or becoming a community police officer. It could be helping out within your religious community or 12-Step fellowship and/or using your skills or a sport to raise money for charity.

- *Miscellaneous hobbies* – these are activities that don't fit into the other lists, such as astronomy, astrology, bird-watching, drone-flying, karting, flying, gliding, learning a language, bee-keeping, falconry, horse riding, ancestry, flower-arranging, computing, electronics, car mechanics, magic arts, mindfulness, memory training, ecology, aromatherapy – I'm sure there are many more. If there is something new you think you'd be interested in, search online and see what courses are available in your area or what courses and clubs you can join online.

I'm sure there are many, many things I've forgotten, but I hope this list will have inspired you to think about activities you'd like to explore. All of these activities have the potential of giving you a healthier and more balanced lifestyle, but that doesn't mean you won't occasionally experience difficult emotions and part of secure recovery means having strategies for handling those when they occur.

Managing emotions

There's a well-known saying in recovery – 'the good news is you get your feelings back, but the bad news is you get your feelings back.' As the anaesthetic of acting out wears off, emotions are re-awakened and some of those will be uncomfortable, or even painful. Getting into recovery means being comfortable with feeling and expressing the full range of emotions and one of the ways many people do that is by developing their emotional intelligence.

The term 'emotional intelligence' has been buzzing around and growing in popularity since the early 1980s and the majority of people now accept the importance of the concept. Emotional intelligence is essential for navigating relationships and developing the lifestyle that we desire. There are dozens of different definitions of EI but they all basically boil down to this: 'Emotional Intelligence is the ability to identify, understand, manage and take appropriate action on the emotions of self and others.' It's easy to see that someone with good emotional intelligence will be in a stronger position to determine their own destiny, communicate with others and avoid coercion. And if, or perhaps when, hardship strikes they'll also be equipped to healthily manage and express their feelings and gain the support of others. EI is a skill that some seem to be born with, whereas others have to learn and develop it.

The first requirement of emotional intelligence is to learn to identify our emotional needs. In the world of emotional intelligence this is known as emotional literacy and it's a notion that has been embraced by workers with young people where it's been proven that learning a language of emotion helps young people's mental stability. When a teenager is taught the language to recognise and express their rage they're less inclined to hit out physically. And when they can differentiate between their feelings of fear, sadness and frustration they can consider their options and make a decision about the best course of action to take.

Once we have identified and named our emotional needs, including any underlying primary needs, we can begin to understand them. Once we know *how* we feel we can ask *why* we feel. In the realms of emotional intelligence this is where someone, having recognised their feelings of anger or sadness or fear, might ask themselves what has caused that emotion. What is going on in their inner and outer world that has evoked this emotional state?

How we manage our emotional feelings is essential, not only for our own sense of self-worth, autonomy and personal satisfaction, but also for our relationships and our society. When emotions are out of control, they affect those around us. It's easy to see how uncontrolled anger and, to a certain extent, sadness and pessimism can have a negative effect. But positive feeling states such as happiness can also have a significant impact. Being around someone who is overflowing with happiness may inspire you to be happy, or it may make you feel more miserable by comparison, or even irritated. That's not to say that managing our emotion will mean that we keep it hidden but we should be aware of its impact and therefore ensure that its communication is within our control.

As explored in previous chapters, all addictions are a method of emotional regulation. They either create a positive emotion or eliminate a negative one. Increasing emotional intelligence can help us establish confident recovery by becoming better at identifying, understanding, managing and expressing emotion. All of us have some emotions that are harder to manage than others and these will probably be the very ones that someone with an addiction will be left struggling with once the anaesthetic has been removed. Individual therapy, as well as being a member of a recovery community, offers a great place to develop and practice emotional intelligence.

Developing assertiveness

Closely associated to managing emotion, and equally important, is developing the ability to assert our own needs and, regrettably, one of the casualties of shame is loss of assertiveness. As sex and porn addiction slowly erodes self-esteem, many sufferers lose their capacity to stand up for themselves and say how they feel and what they need. Many feel they have lost the right to assert themselves and drift into passivity and inertia. A few swing the other way towards aggression. A common defence mechanism against shame is grandiosity and self-entitlement and this means that some people in recovery become overly demanding and aggressive. It's important to recognise that being assertive is not about putting your needs ahead of someone else's, but putting them on an equal level. It is about respecting self and others.

Developing assertiveness is essential for maintaining a balanced and fulfilling life. When we're assertive we're able to express our opinions and feelings, say 'no' without feeling guilty and prioritise our time to fit with our values and needs. Without assertiveness we're likely to say 'Yes' to things that we don't want to do and put up with situations that are unfair. The result is a life that is governed by others' needs and desires, rather than our own. Lack of assertiveness also damages intimacy in relationships as real needs and feelings are suppressed and partners, friends and family may never get to know the real person. For someone recovering from addiction it is particularly important to learn assertiveness so that needs and emotions that were previously soothed by the addiction are managed healthily.

The first task in developing assertiveness is to identify the times and places where being assertive is a problem. Once identified, the thoughts and cognitive distortions that block assertiveness can then be explored. For example, someone might recognise that they don't ever say no to friends because they fear they won't be liked. Or they don't ask their partner for more time alone because they fear it would hurt their feelings or turn into an argument. These thoughts can then be tested for their validity and either reframed or taken into account. Like emotional intelligence, these skills are often most usefully learnt in individual therapy and within a recovery community.

Overcoming blocks to recovery

Unfortunately, addiction is often not an easy problem to overcome and some people will experience slips, or even relapses, along the way, but continuing relapses, or even escalation, indicate a deeper problem.

Some will have left acting out behaviours firmly in the past, but recovery continues to feel like a drudge rather than a pleasure. In both of these instances the most likely cause is that an underlying block has either not yet been recognised, or not yet resolved.

The most common block is an unresolved psychological issue, as explored in Chapter 3, or a faulty core belief, discussed in Chapter 10. Until the deeper causes of sex and porn addiction are dealt with, an anaesthetic will still be sought. If someone has a complex trauma and attachment-induced addiction then it may take years of therapy to resolve the underlying problem. Although a cognitive understanding of the problem may have been reached, this knowledge takes time to filter into emotions, which can leave recovery feeling like an empty reward. Or if some acting out continues, each slip may reinforce negative emotions and hence create more triggers and continue the cycle of addiction.

Another common block is lack of motivation or commitment to change, and most often this is the result of not having developed a better vision for the future (Chapter 11) or identified, and enjoyed, positive sexuality (Chapter 13). However, even the most committed person may find that their motivation wavers if they continue to experience slips or relapse. One of the slogans of the 12-Step movement is 'progress not perfection' – absorbing the truth of this statement can help someone to get back on the wagon again. In this final section we explore two other possible blocks to recovery.

Unforgiveness

Throughout this book I have talked about how shame is one of the biggest problems people with sex and porn addiction have to face and overcome. When shame has not been overcome, unforgiveness will inevitably take hold and can rob a person of any sense of deserving to recover. Unforgiveness may be of the self or it may be a partner who refuses to forgive. When this happens it is impossible to escape the regret phase of the cycle. And even though acting out may have stopped a long time ago, and triggers may be healthily managed, someone who remains unforgiven, remains trapped in the cycle of addiction.

Framing forgiveness as an essential part of recovery can, in itself, give permission for forgiveness to begin, but many feel that to forgive themselves, or expect a partner to forgive, would be synonymous with saying what happened didn't matter. Forgiveness is often wrongly perceived as being 'let off the hook' and some feel that being constantly reminded of the pain that's been caused is a price they must pay.

Withholding forgiveness is often used as a punishment and in these situations the person with the addiction remains accused of their crime and must continue to suffer lest they reoffend. In reality, the opposite is more probable, as suffering is much more likely to trigger addiction than forgiveness. Forgiveness does not mean that the crime will be forgotten or that work on rebuilding relationships and self-esteem has been concluded. On the contrary, it makes space and frees energy for that work to begin.

Forgiveness is easy to talk about but much, much harder to do. The first step is to understand and recognise the benefits of forgiveness and then decide if you want to forgive. When it is a partner who cannot forgive, they can be helped to recognise that the key benefit of forgiving will be for themselves, to 'let themselves off the hook' of anger and bitterness – there's much more on this in Sex Addiction – The Partner's Perspective (tbc). Forgiving yourself is usually harder than forgiving someone else. When asked, most people agree that if a friend had this addiction and had done the same things, they would not hesitate to forgive.

It can be helpful to explore the pros and cons of forgiveness and also break down precisely what needs to be forgiven. For example, it may be easier to forgive yourself for some behaviours, but not others; or to forgive yourself for some of the deceits but not others. Regrettably whilst there continues to be a lack of education about sex and porn addiction as well as a lack of qualified treatment services, I hope that most can forgive themselves for not recognising they had an addiction and seeking help sooner.

Forgiveness is a process, not a one-off event. It takes time, but the sooner you can forgive yourself and accept the forgiveness of others, the sooner self-esteem will grow and recovery can be fully claimed and enjoyed.

Opportunity

The last, but by no means the least, block to recovery is the ultimate enemy, opportunity. Many people with sex and porn addiction talk about going months or even years without a craving or without even thinking about their addiction, until opportunity came and knocked at their door. The house is empty and someone has left their unprotected laptop sitting on the side. Or a meeting is cancelled and you're alone in a town where you know a sex worker is just a phone call or text away. Or a beautiful stranger approaches you, or pings you a message, and it's obvious that no-strings-attached sex is on the agenda. When opportunity strikes, resolve can disappear out of the window and endless cognitive distortions can flood the mind, along with euphoric recall of how fantastic acting out used to feel. For some, this may result in acting out, and for many this can leave them feeling that their recovery is not as good as they thought it was. It's essential to remember that being tempted and being triggered is not the same as acting out. As long as you don't act out, then your recovery is intact. If there are repeated temptations, then it's wise to double up on recovery activities, as we've discussed earlier in this chapter, connect with others and perhaps get back to therapy or 12-Step meetings or a recovery group. Opportunity will always be there, which means triggers will be as well, but acting on those triggers can permanently become a thing of the past. It's your choice.

And so it seems we have come full circle from the start of this book. We undoubtedly live in a world where there is more sexual freedom and opportunity than at any other time on earth. The Internet provides us with endless variety and unlimited access to sexual exploration. Progressive social standards accept a range of sexual lifestyles, some of which are profoundly challenging to those who struggle with sex or porn addiction. Ultimately, recovering from addiction is a choice, a daily choice, to overcome childhood difficulties, triggers, urges and blocks and develop healthy relationships, positive sexuality and a fulfilling lifestyle

References

Csikszentmihalyi, M. (2002) *Flow*, Rider, London.
Hall, P. (2015) *Sex Addiction: The Partner's Perspective*, London, Routledge.
Melemis, S.M. (2010) *I want to change my life*, Modern Therapies, Toronto.

Conclusion

Sex and porn addiction are devastating conditions that affect many millions of innocent people. Not just those who personally struggle with them, but also those who love them. Relationships and families can be torn apart, jobs lost, health and personal values compromised and self-esteem left in tatters. It is my belief that addiction can be overcome completely, if you 'choose' to, but recovery is a lifelong process of beating triggers, maintaining integrity and claiming life.

My hope is that this book will have gone some way to increasing understanding of both sex and porn addiction and thereby raising compassion and generating hope, and that the exercises provided within these pages will help to provide both a compass and a map to full recovery.

The serenity prayer, first composed by theologian Reinhold Niebuhr and adopted by the 12-Step community, sums up both the struggle and the solution for all in addiction recovery. And indeed, for all who strive to manage the complexities of life. We must all learn to accept that there are things in life that we will never be able to change, and find the courage to 'choose' to change the things that are our responsibility.

> God, grant me the Serenity to
> Accept the things I cannot change,
> the Courage to change the things I can,
> and the Wisdom to know the difference.
>
> Amen.

Further reading and resources

Books about sex and porn addiction

CBT for Compulsive Sexual Behaviour, A Guide for Professionals, Thaddeus Birchard (Routledge).
Counselling Male Sexual Offenders: A Strength-Focused Approach, London, Andrew Smith (Routledge).
Confronting Porn, A Guide for Christians, Paula Hall, (Naked Truth Resources).
Cruise Control – Understanding Sex Addiction in Gay Men, Robert Weiss, (Alyson Publications Inc).
Facing Love Addiction: giving yourself the power to change the way you love, Pia Mellody (Harper One).
Freedom from our Addictions, Russell Brand (Bluebird Books).
In the Shadows of the Net – Breaking Free from Compulsive Online Sexual Behaviour, Patrick Carnes, David Delmonico & Elizabeth Griffin (Hazelden).
Making Advances: A Comprehensive Guide for Treating Female Sex and Love Addicts, Marnie Ferree (SASH).
Out of the Doghouse – A Step by Step Relationship-Saving Guide for men caught cheating, Robert Weiss (Health Communications Inc).
Out of the Shadows – Understanding Sex Addiction, Patrick Carnes (Hazelden).
Overcoming Sex Addiction, A Self-Help Guide, Thaddeus Birchard (Routledge).
Sex Addiction 101 – The Workbook, Robert Weiss (Health Communications Inc).
The Routledge International Handbook of Sexual Addiction, edited by Thaddeus 19 Birchard & Joanna Benfield (Routledge).
Sex Addiction as Affect Dysregulation, A Neurobiologically Informed Holistic Treatment, Alexandra Katehakis (Norton).

Sex Addiction Cure: How to Overcome Porn Addiction and Sexual Compulsion, Matt Peplinski, (Psycho Tao).
Sexual Addiction – An Integrated Approach, Aviel Goodman (International Universities Press).
Sex Addiction 101 – A basic guide to healing from sex, porn, and love addiction, Robert Weiss (Health Communications Inc).
Something for the weekend, Life in the Chemsex Underworld, J. Wharton (Biteback Publishing).
The Porn Trap – The Essential Guide to Overcoming Problems caused by Pornography, Wendy Maltz & Larry Maltz, (Harper).
Treating Out of Control Sexual Behaviour: Rethinking Sex Addiction, Doug Braun-Harvey (Springer Publishing Company).
Untangling the Web – Sex, Porn and Fantasy Obsession in the Internet Age, Robert Weiss, Jennifer Schneider (Alyson Books).
Your Brain on Porn, Internet pornography and the emerging science of addiction, Gary Wilson (Commonwealth Publishing).

Books for partners

Is My Husband Gay, Straight or Bi? A Guide for Women Concerned About Their Man, Joe Kort (Rowman and Littlefield).
Mending a Shattered Heart – A Guide for Partners of Sex Addicts, edited by Stefanie Carnes (Gentle Path Press).
Sex Addiction – A Guide for Partners, Paula Hall (Routledge).
Your Sexually Addicted Spouse, Barbara Steffens and Martha Means (New Horizon Press).

Books about general psychology and self help

Authentic Happiness, Martin Seligman (Nicholas Brealey).
Daring Greatly. How the Courage to be Vulnerable Transforms the Way We Live, Love, Parent and Lead, Brene Brown (Penguin).
Emotional Intelligence – Why it Can Matter More than IQ, Daniel Goleman (Bloomsbury).
I want to Change my Life, Stephen Melemis (Modern Therapies).
Infant Losses, Adult Searches – A neural and Developmental perspective on psychopathology and sexual offending, Glyn Hudson Allez, (Karnac).
No More Mr Nice Guy, A Proven Plan for Getting What You Want in Love, Sex and Life, Robert Glover (Barnes & Noble).
Rewriting the Rules – A New Guide to Love, Sex and Relationships, Meg Barker (Routledge).

The Body Remembers – A Psychophysiology of Trauma and Trauma Treatment, Babette Rothschild (Norton).
The Chimp Paradox: the mind management programme, Steve Peters (Vermillion).
The Mindful Brain, Daniel Siegel (Norton).
Waking the Tiger: Healing Trauma, Peter Levine (North Atlantic Books).
Wherever You Go, There You Are, Jon Kabat-Zinn (Hearst Publications).

Additional resources

ATSAC (Association for the Treatment of Sexual Addiction and Compulsivity).The UK's professional association for sex addiction professionals. www.atsac.co.uk

Fight the New Drug – a free online recovery programme for adolescents and adults struggling with porn addiction. https://fortifyprogram.org

ISAT (Institute for Sex Addiction Training) – Accredited diploma training and CPD for professionals in Sex and Porn Addiction. www.thelaurelcentre.co.uk/sex-addiction-training

Kick Start Recovery Programme – A free online resource created by Paula Hall to help individuals struggling with sex and porn addiction. www.sexaddictionhelp.co.uk

The Laurel Centre – International services for Recovery and Support for Partners developed by Paula Hall. www.thelaurelcentre.co.uk

The Naked Truth Project – a national charity providing resources and services for porn recovery and education for parents and pastoral carers. www.thenakedtruthproject.com

Recovery Nation – a free online resource for addicts, partners and couples. www.recoverynation.com

SAA (Sex Addicts Anonymous). www.saa-recovery.org.uk

SLAA (Sex and Love Addicts Anonymous). www.slaauk.org

StopSo, Specialist Treatment Organisation for the Prevention of Sex Offending, info@stopso.org.uk.

Your Brain on Porn – A science based website that provides information about the impact of pornography and recovery advice for those whose porn use is a problem. www.yourbrainonporn.com

Index

Italic page numbers indicate tables; bold indicate figures.

12-Step fellowships 90, 173–175
12-Step programme 93, 107, 120, 166, 174

abandonment, fear of 74
abstinence 156
abuse: abusive parenting 46; origins of addiction 41–42
acceptance 168
Acceptance and Commitment Therapy (ACT) 115–116, 145
access restriction 145–146
acting out 12, 55–57, 138
addiction: consequences of 14–18, *16*; existence of 5–6; functions of 11–12; impact of 17–18; as moral issue 5; neurochemistry of 12–14; risks of 16; use of term 8
addiction models 9
adolescents: assessment 30; loneliness 39–40; shame 38–39
Alexander, B. 165
alternative names 9
altruism 125
ambivalent attachment 167, 168
anxious attachment 166–168
assault 42
assertiveness 186
assessment: adolescents 30; attachment-induced addiction 26–27, 28–29; behaviour table *24*; classification 25–29; context and overview 21–22; defining types of addiction 28–29; gender, sexual and relationship diverse clients 30–31; heteronormative bias 30–31; and mental health disorders 31; opportunity-induced addiction 25–26, 28; and other addictions 31; process 22–25; Questionnaire 1 22–23; Questionnaire 2 23–25; trauma-induced addiction 27–28, 29
attachment: and love addiction 74; and mental health 166; neuroscience of 45–46; styles 166–168
attachment-induced addiction 26–27, 28–29; acting out 56–57; core beliefs 113; dormant phase 53; origins of addiction 45–47; preparation phase 54–55; triggers 53, 128–129, 132–133
attentional bias 13–14
avoidant attachment 167, 168

balanced life 122–126
BDSM (Bondage, Domination, Submission, Masochism) 97
behavioural addictions 8
belief systems 112, 155–156; *see also* core beliefs
BERSC model 34–35, **35**, 49
biopsychosocial model 34
Birchard, T. 114
bisexual people 80

blame 135
boat metaphor 67
book: aims and scope 1–2; chapter summaries 3; reflection and conclusion 190
boundaries, decision making and self-control 152
broadcasting 183

Carnes, P. 7, 112
celibacy 157, 160–161
change: inability to 112–114; resistance to 111–112
changing: core beliefs 115–116; environmental 146–147
chapter summaries 3
chemical addictions 8
chemsex 84–86
childhood issues 150–151
choice: recovery as 108; shame as 116
C.H.O.I.C.E. Recovery Model: overview 2, 105; *see also* compulsive behaviours; connecting with others; core beliefs; positive sexuality; recovery; vision
circle exercise 156–158, **157**
classical conditioning 144
classification 25–29
co-dependency 65
Cognitive Behavioural Therapy (CBT) 112
cognitive distortions 54–55, *55*, 58, 94, 108, 115, 128, 134–136
community work 183–184
co-morbidity, and assessment 31
compulsive behaviours: accepting triggers and craving 144–145; acting out 138, *139*; childhood issues 150–151; context and overview 128–130; cycles of addiction 128–129; decision making, boundaries and self-control 152; distraction 148–149; dormant phase 130–131; environmental change 146–147; looking the other way 146; managing negative emotions 151–152; neuroscience 144; preparation phase 134–137; reconstitution 141–142; regret phase 138, 140; relapse prevention 143–149; restriction of access 145–146; R.U.N. 147–148; Seemingly Unimportant Decisions (S.U.D.s) 136–137; short, sharp shocks 148; stopping the cycle 142–143; time management 147; trigger phase 131–134; triggers 131–134; underlying issues 149–152; understanding triggers and craving 143–144
concentric circle exercise **170**
confidentiality, sex offending 100–101
confirmation of experience 168
connecting with others: 12-Step fellowships 173–175; attachment styles 166–168; concentric circle exercise **170**; context and overview 165–166; couple relationships 169; as daily discipline 179; families 171; friendships 170; reasons for 166–169; relational needs 168–169; support groups 175; therapeutic recovery groups 171–173; *see also* partners and relationships; relationships
consequences, of addiction 14–18, *16*, 108–110
contribution, balanced life 125
co-occurring addictions 31
coping mechanisms 11–12
core beliefs: changing 115–116; context and overview 107; denial 107–111; formation 113; impact on self-esteem 113–114; inability to change 112–114; resistance to change 111–112; shame 114–115; *see also* underlying issues
costs, of addiction 8, 14–18, 109
couple relationships 169; impact of addiction 65–67
Craig 130; childhood issues 151; decision making, boundaries and self-control 152; managing negative emotions 152; six-phase cycle **131**, **134**, 137, **137**, **140**, **142**
craving: accepting 144–145; understanding 143–144
creativity 183
Criminal Justice Act 97

Criminal Justice and Immigration Act 2008 97
cross-addiction 31
crystal meth 84
CSA images 97; and confidentiality 100; risk assessment 101–102
cyber flashing 97–98
cycle of reaction 64
cycles of addiction 50–59, 128–129

daily disciplines 178–181
dating 157–158
deceit 107
decision making: boundaries and self-control 152; value-based 121
definitions: alternative names 9; comparators 7; consequences of addiction 14–18, *16*; context and overview 5; desire and addiction 7–8; features of 6–8; functions of addiction 11–12; impact of addiction 17–18; love addiction 10–11; mood altering 12; neurochemistry of addiction 12–14; porn addiction 10; reality of addiction 8–10; relationship with behaviours 6–7; risks of addiction *16*; role of dopamine 12–14; use of terms 9; variations of addiction 10–11
denial 21–22, 107–111, 136
dependency, as defining factor 6
desire, and addiction 7–8
diagnosis: criteria and acceptance of 8–9; as determinism 9
Diagnostic and Statistical Manual of the American Psychiatric Association (DSM) 8, 83
diet 180
disclosure, impact of 63
distraction 148–149
distress 83
dopamine 12–14
dormant phase 52–53, 130–131
double standards 77
drug use 84–86

Earp, D. 73
eating disorders 7
emotional abuse 41

emotional control 150
emotional intelligence 184–185
emotional pain management 56
emotional reactions, partners 61–62
emotional regulation 130–131
emotional relapse 176–177
emotional self-management 37
emotion management 184–185
emotions, negative 151–152
empathy 125
Engel, G. 34
enmeshment 74
entitlement 135
environmental change 146–147
erectile difficulties 163
Erskine, R.G. 168
escape 7
ethics 100–101
eulogy exercise 122
exercise, for health and wellbeing 180
exercises: acting out 139; circle exercise 156–158, **157**; cognitive distortions 134–136; consequences of addiction 108–110; emotional regulation 130–131; faulty core beliefs 114; life wheel 125–126; reconstitution 141; regret phase 140; risks of addiction 110–111; Seemingly Unimportant Decisions (S.U.D.s) 137; triggers 132–133; values 120; writing a vision 122
exhibitionism 97–98
extreme pornography 97

facing the future 64
faith communities and spirituality: 12-Step programme 93; cognitive distortions 94; consequences of addiction 94; context and overview 90; hypocrisy 94; positive sexuality 95; religion and addiction 91–92; spirituality and addiction 90–91; spiritual recovery tools 95; working with people from faith communities 93–94
families 171; balanced life 123
fantasies 161
fear of abandonment 74
fear of intimacy 74
Ferree, M.C. 74

financial effects 15
flow 182
FLSA (Female Sex & Love Addiction): context and overview 73; defining love addition 73–75; porn addiction 75–77; sexuality 76, 77; shame 77; socialisation 76, 77; treatment regimes 77; triggers 77; working with women 75–77
forgiveness 187–188
Fossum, M.A. 50
friendships 170; balanced life 123; concentric circle exercise **170**
functions, of addiction 11–12
fun/recreation 123–124
further reading: general 191–192; partners and relationships 192; psychology/self-help 192–193

gay men 80
gender, sexual and relationship diversity (GSRD) communities: chemsex 84–86; context and overview 79; gay, lesbian and bisexual 79–80; hypervigilance 87; impact on partners 62; internalised heterosexism 87; kink 82–84; minority stress 87; MSM (Men who have Sex with Men) 80–82; religion 87–88; sexual health 88; spirituality 87–88; therapeutic approaches 86–88; use of terms 79
Geoff 111–112
getting away with it 108
GHB/GBL 84
goal setting 126–127
gratitude 181
group work 171–173
guilt 115

Hall, P. 10, 25, 30, 34, 49, 51, 98
Hall Recovery Course 171–173
happiness 122
Hari, J. 165
health, daily disciplines 179–180
health effects 15; gender, sexual and relationship diversity (GSRD) communities 88
healthy attachment 45
healthy pursuits and pastimes 182–184

helplessness 136
help seeking 21
heritage and culture 183
heteronormative bias 30–31
hobbies 184
homophobia 82
hyper-arousal 56, **56**
hypervigilance, gender, sexual and relationship diversity (GSRD) communities 87
hypo-arousal 56, **56**
hypocrisy 94

illegal online images 97
impact of addiction 17–18
inability to change 112–114
inadequate parenting 46
indecency, defining 97
initiating, shared 168
internalised heterosexism 87
International Classification of Diseases (ICD) 9
Internet, effects of 6, 26, 35
intimacy: fear of 74; partners and relationships 66–67
invincibility 136
Is My Husband Gay, Straight or Bi (Kort) 81
isolation 175

journaling 180–181
justification 135

Kabat-Zinn, J. 64
Kasl, C.S. 80
kink 82–84, 97
Kort, J. 81

labelling, effects of 9, 21–22
lesbian women 79–80
Ley, D. 90
libido 156
life events, origins of addiction 42–43
life paths, fragility of 34
lifestyle evaluation 122–127
life wheel 125–126, **125**
loneliness 39–40, 175
looking the other way 146
loss 111

love addiction: defining 73–75; overview 10
love, giving 169
low sexual desire 162

Madonna/whore syndrome 162
magnifying 135
maintenance and reinforcement: acting out 55–57; BERSC model 49; cognitive distortions 54–55, *55*; context and overview 49; cycles of addiction 50–59; dormant phase 52–53; neuroscience of 49; oscillating release/control cycle 50–51, *50*; preparation phase 54–55; reconstitution 58; regret phase 57–58; six-phase cycle 51–58, *51*; triggers 53
managing emotions 184–185
managing negative emotions 151–152
Mason, M.J. 50
masturbation, mindful 163–164
Melemis, S. 176
Mellody, P. 74
menstruation 76, 77
mental filtering 135–136
mental health disorders, and assessment 31
mental relapse 177
mephedrone 84
Merton, T. 122
mindful masturbation 163–164
minimisation 108, 135
minority stress 87
models of addiction 9
monogamous couples, and sex 158
mood altering 12
moral debate 5
moral judgement 154
Motivational Interviewing 112, 115
MSM (Men who have Sex with Men) 80–82
music 183

nature and outdoor activities 183
negative emotions 151–152
negative thinking patterns 112–113
negligent parenting 46
neurochemistry, of addiction 12–14

Neuro Linguistic Programming (NLP) 149
neuroscience: of attachment 45–46; of maintenance and reinforcement 49; of trauma 43–44; triggers 144
Niebuhr, R. 190
normalisation 136

OAT Model 25–29, **26**
online sex-offending *see* sex offending
open non-monogamous relationships 159–160
opportunity, as challenge to recovery 188
opportunity-induced addiction 25–26, 28; core beliefs 113; dormant phase 52–53; origins of addiction 35–40; triggers 53, 128, 132
orgasmic disorders 163
origins of addiction: abuse 41–42; assault 42; attachment and the brain 45–46; attachment-induced addiction 45–47; BERSC model 34–35, **35**; context and overview 33–35; emotional self-management 37; impact of trauma 43–44; loneliness 39–40; opportunity-induced addiction 35–40; parenting styles 46; questions 33, 34; secrecy 37–38; self-control 36–37; sex education 38–39; shame 38; trauma-induced addiction 41–44; traumatic life events 42–43
oscillating release/control cycle 50–51, *50*
others, impact on 168

paraphilias, use of term 83
parenting 36–37; styles 46
partners and relationships: and addiction recovery 68–69; balanced life 123; co-dependency 65; context and overview 61; couple relationships 169; facing the future 64; families 171; friendships 170; further reading 192; gender, sexual and relationship diversity (GSRD) communities 62; impact of

disclosure 63; impact on couple relationships 65–67; impact on partners 61–63; intimacy 66–67; partners' recovery 63–65; recovery 67; relational trauma model 65; reparation of self-identity and esteem 64; sexual intimacy 66–67; SURF 63–64; survival 64; trust 65–66; understanding cycle of reaction 64; *see also* connecting with others; relationships
partners' recovery 63–65
personal experiences: Bill 46; Craig 130, **131**, **134**, **137**, **140**, 142, **142**, 151, 152; Geoff 111–112; impact of addiction 17–18; Mike 40; Peter 44; therapeutic recovery groups 172–173; Tim 59; values 119–120
personal growth, balanced life 124
physical abuse 41
physical relapse 177
porn addiction: female 75–77; overview 10
pornography, extreme 97
positive sexuality 95; belief systems 155–156; celibacy 160–161; circle exercise 156–158, **157**; context and overview 153; defining 154–155; erectile difficulties 163; fantasies 161; identifying sexual messages 155–156; learning about sex 155; low sexual desire 162; mindful masturbation 163–164; monogamous couples 158; open non-monogamous relationships 159–160; orgasmic disorders 163; sexual boundaries 156–158; sexual challenges 161–164; sexual dysfunctions 162–163; sexual frustration 161–162; singles 157–158; *see also* sexuality
powerlessness 107–108
preparation phase 54–55, 134–137
profiling 25
prosecution, effects of 103
Protection of Children Act 97
psycho-education 112
psychology/self-help, further reading 192–193
pursuits and pastimes 182–184

Questionnaire 1 22–23
Questionnaire 2 23–25

rationalisation 134
rat park experiment 165
reading 183
reconstitution 58, 141–142
recovery: assertiveness 186; blocks to 186–189; challenge of opportunity 188; as choice 108; commitment to 118; context and overview 176; daily disciplines 178–181; flow 182; forgiveness 187–188; healthy pursuits and pastimes 182–184; managing emotions 184–185; partners' 63–65; partners and relationships 67; role of partners/relationships 68–69; sexual challenges 161–164; slips (Short Lapses In Progress) 178; stages of relapse 176–177; understanding relapse 176–178; *see also* positive sexuality
regret phase 57–58, 138, 140
reinforcement *see* maintenance and reinforcement
relapse: stages 176–177; understanding 176–178
relapse prevention 143–149; accepting triggers and craving 144–145; childhood issues 150–151; decision making, boundaries and self-control 152; distraction 148–149; environmental change 146–147; looking the other way 146; managing negative emotions 151–152; resolving underlying issues 149–152; restriction of access 145–146; R.U.N. 147–148; short, sharp shocks 148; time management 147; understanding triggers and craving 144–145
relational trauma model 65
relationship effects 15
relationships: as mirrors 166; therapist/client 116; *see also* connecting with others; partners and relationships
relaxation 180; balanced life 124
religion: and addiction 91–92; gender, sexual and relationship diversity

Index

(GSRD) communities 87–88; *see also* faith communities and spirituality
resilience 108
resistance to change 111–112
resources 193
rest, balanced life 124
restriction of access 145–146
risk assessment, sex offending 101–102
risks of addiction 16, 110–111
risk taking 57
rock bottom 108–109
Royal College of Psychiatrists 91
R.U.N. 147–148

secrecy 14–15; origins of addiction 37–38; and shame 116
secure attachment 167
security 168
seeking help 21
Seemingly Unimportant Decisions (S.U.D.s) 54–55, 136–137
self-care 177–178
self-confidence 113
self-control 36–37; boundaries and decision making 152
self-definition 168
self-doubt 113
self-esteem: effects of addiction 15–16, 57–58; impact of core beliefs 113–114; partners' 64; repairing 58
self-identity, partners' 64
separation, and attachment 46
sex: learning about 155; monogamous couples 158; open non-monogamous relationships 159–160; singles 157–158
Sex & Love Addicts Anonymous (SLAA) 173, 177
Sex Addiction – A Guide for Couples (Hall) 67
Sex Addiction Severity Assessment Tool (SASAT) 23–25
Sex Addiction – The Partner's Perspective (Hall) 63
Sex Addicts Anonymous (SAA) 12, 173, 177
Sexaholics Anonymous (SA) 175, 177

sex drive, and addiction 7–8
sex education 38–39
sex offending: causes/reasons for 98–99; confidentiality 100–101; context and overview 96; defining 96–98; effects of prosecution 103; and ethics 100–101; exhibitionism 97–98; nature of 96–97; online 96–97; reactions to 96; risk assessment 101–102; sentencing 98; therapeutic approaches 102–103; voyeurism 97–98
sexual abuse 42, 81
sexual assault, chemsex 86
sexual boundaries 156–158
sexual challenges 161–164; fantasies 161; sexual dysfunctions 162–163; sexual frustration 161–162
sexual dysfunctions 162–163
sexual frustration 161–162
sexual health, gender, sexual and relationship diversity (GSRD) communities 88
sexual identity, MSM (Men who have Sex with Men) 81
sexual intimacy, partners and relationships 66–67
sexuality: expression of 1; power of 1; use of term 154; women 76, 77; *see also* positive sexuality
sexually-transmitted infections (STIs) 15
sexual messages 155–156
shame 38, 57–58, 77, 112, 114–117
short, sharp shocks 148
shyness 39–40
sin 92
singles, and sex 157–158
six-phase cycle 51–58, *51*, 128ff, **129, 131, 134, 137, 138, 140, 142**; accepting triggers and craving 144–145; acting out 55–57, 138, 139; cognitive distortions 54–55, *55*; dormant phase 52–53, 130–131; phases 52; preparation phase 54–55, 134–137; reconstitution 58, 141–142; regret phase 57–58, 138, 140; relapse prevention 143–149; stopping the cycle 142–143; triggers 53, 131–134
sleep 179–180

slips (Short Lapses In Progress) 178
SMART goals 126–127
smart phones, effects of 6
social costs 8
socialisation, women 76, 77
socio-cultural differences, overview 71
Soloman, R. 43
Something for the Weekend (Wharton) 85
spiritual exercises 181
spiritual health 90
spirituality: and addiction 90–91; defining 90–91; gender, sexual and relationship diversity (GSRD) communities 87–88; *see also* faith communities and spirituality
spiritual recovery tools 95
sport and fitness 183
stigma 9; women 75–76
stopping the cycle 142–143
Supernormal Stimuli 26
support groups 175
SURF 63–64
survival 64

technology, effects of 6
The Bubble 12
The Chemsex Study (Bourne *et al.*) 85–86
The Opponent Process Theory of Acquired Motivation 43
therapeutic alliances 102
therapeutic approaches: gender, sexual and relationship diversity (GSRD) communities 86–88; sex offending 102–103
therapeutic recovery groups 171–173
therapist/client relationship 116
The Serenity Prayer 182, 190
time management 147
Tina (crystal meth) 84
Transactional Analysis 115–116, 124
trauma, impact of 43–44
trauma-induced addiction 27–28, 29; acting out 56–57; core beliefs 113; dormant phase 53; origins of addiction 41–44; preparation phase 54–55; regret phase 57–58; triggers 53, 128, 133

traumatic life events, origins of addiction 42–43
treatment regimes, FLSA (Female Sex & Love Addiction) 77
triggers 53, 131–134; accepting 144; attachment-induced addiction 53, 132–133; FLSA (Female Sex & Love Addiction) 77; managing 149; neuroscience 144; opportunity-induced addiction 53, 128, 132; trauma-induced addiction 53, 128, 133; understanding 143–144
trust, partners and relationships 65–66

underlying issues 149–152; childhood issues 150–151; *see also* core beliefs
understanding triggers and craving 143–144
unforgiveness 187–188
Unholy Trinity 84
uniqueness 135
up skirting 97–98
use of terms 1, 8, 9–10, 79, 82–83

validation 168
value-based decision making 121
values, establishing 118–121
variations of addiction 10–11
Viagra 84
victim stance 136
vision: balanced life 122–126; context and overview 118; creating 121–122; establishing values 118–121; goal setting 126–127; importance of 128; lifestyle evaluation 122–127; value-based decision making 121; writing 122
voyeurism 97–98

well being 90
Wharton, J. 85
Wilson, B. 93
withdrawal, effects of 14, 145
women: sexuality 76, 77; shame 77; socialisation 76, 77; stigma 75–76; *see also* FLSA (Female Sex & Love Addiction)
work, balanced life 124
World Health Authority 90

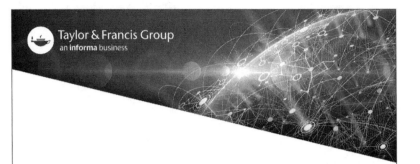